THE BOOK OF KIN

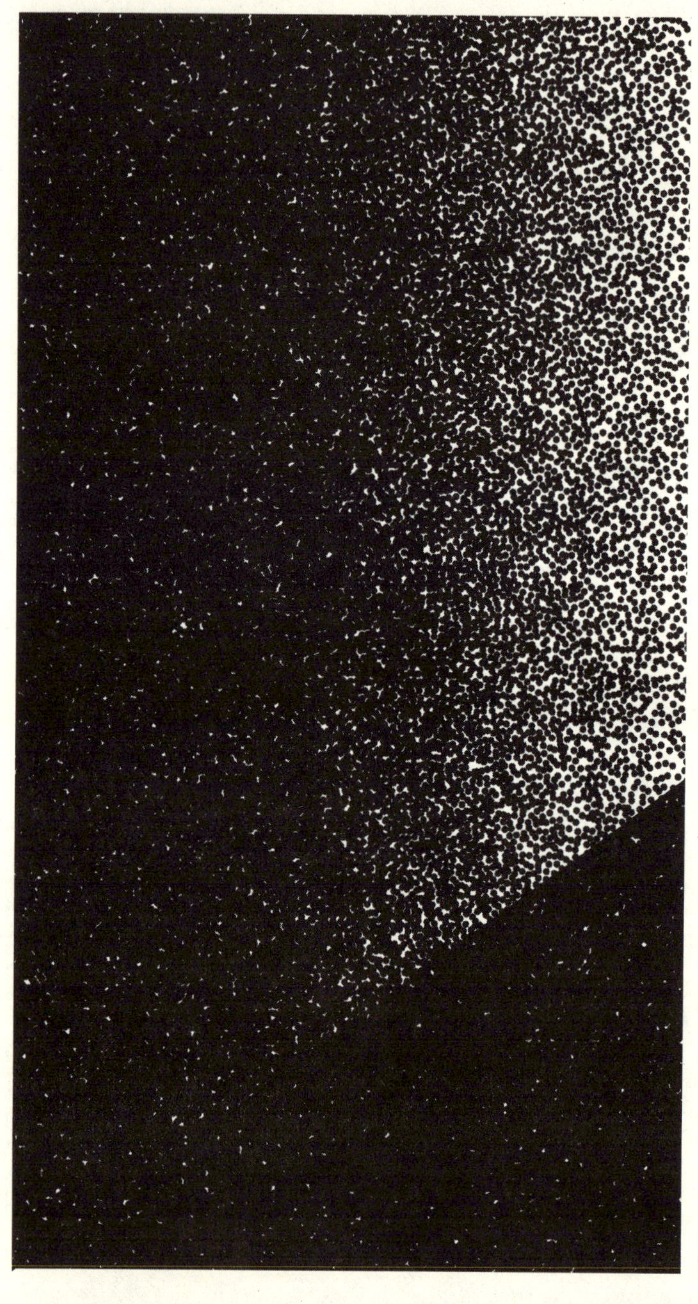

THE BOOK OF KIN

On Absence, Love, and Being There

JENNIFER ELI BOWEN

MILKWEED EDITIONS

Published 2025 by Milkweed Editions
Printed in Canada
Cover design by Mary Austin Speaker
Author photo by Emily Baxter
25 26 27 28 29 5 4 3 2 1
First Edition

Library of Congress Cataloging-in-Publication Data

Names: Bowen, Jennifer Eli author
Title: The book of kin : on absence, love, and being there / Jennifer Eli Bowen.
Description: Minneapolis, Minnesota : Milkweed Editions, 2025. | Summary: "An urgent debut essay collection examining the effects of abandonment, imprisonment, and care, and how the power of love connects us all"-- Provided by publisher.
Identifiers: LCCN 2025004308 | ISBN 9781571311672 paperback | ISBN 9781571317964 ebook
Subjects: LCGFT: Essays
Classification: LCC PS3602.O89568 B66 2025 | DDC 814/.6--dc23/eng/20250306
LC record available at https://lccn.loc.gov/2025004308

Milkweed Editions is committed to ecological stewardship. We strive to align our book production practices with this principle, and to reduce the impact of our operations in the environment. We are a member of the Green Press Initiative, a nonprofit coalition of publishers, manufacturers, and authors working to protect the world's endangered forests and conserve natural resources. *The Book of Kin* was printed on acid-free 100% postconsumer-waste paper by Friesens Corporation.

For Elliot and Oliver

Contents

AUTHOR'S NOTE

Writing is the way I know to make meaning in this world, but that doesn't mean narrative isn't still a slippery bitch, as able to make whole as to harm. I changed and abbreviated some names for privacy. It's all true, but only my truth, at one moment in time.

We cobble love together
from this and those of our machinery
until there is suddenly an apparition
that never existed before.

—JACK GILBERT

THE BOOK OF KIN

Next of Kin

My dad was dead when I finally introduced him to my husband of seven years. He happened to be in his casket at the time, and through my tears, I said, "Hey, this is Tommy. Tommy, this is B." No, it wasn't ideal.

Then I said to B.—who was still then a young man in a young marriage—"See. I told you I had his hands." I hadn't seen those hands for twenty-odd years. They looked like the hands of a meat-packer, because they were. And I had the hands of a meat-packer's daughter. My mother's hands were slender and feminine, nothing like mine. Her oval-shaped nails were foreign to me. The hands I'd been hiding inside my shirt sleeves since junior high—the hands as masculine as the boys I was hiding them from—those were my dad's.

The funeral would begin soon, but I was reluctant to leave my father's side. As the room filled with people, it struck me that this was my last chance to be with this man I'd never known. He'd missed everything since he and my mother had split more than twenty-five years earlier. Irrationally I'd brought a pile of pictures to the funeral to show him: A photo of Sam, my newborn, purple-red as he greeted the world. Of Leo, my oldest, bright-eyed with his mouth wide open—talking, always talking. Of me rappelling off a cliff with B. at Backbone State Park. Of my sisters and me arm in arm, dressed up, with huge ’80s bangs and glossy lips. I lifted his suit coat and slipped the stack of photos inside his breast pocket.

Then I took a seat in the front row, feeling empty. I looked at him in his coffin and remembered all the times I’d felt he had been watching me from afar, feeling proud. For the first time I was aware of how crazy that was.

The funeral ended, and the priest intoned, “Creator of all the living, we entrust to Your gentle care all those we love who have gone before us; watch over Your son Thomas, Lord.” He raised his hands high in the air as my own son wailed and rooted in my arms, desperate to nurse.

As a young girl I practiced a telepathic system of communication with my dad. So, though he was altogether absent from my life, he was wildly present in my imagination: watching, smiling, and applauding my day-to-day existence.

My mom had given me one brief, well-intentioned narrative about him: “He’s a wonderful man, and very sensitive.” A wonderful, very sensitive man, I thought, would probably love his daughters from afar if they had a new stepfather, especially if this new stepfather had once been his good friend and neighbor. I imagined that my dad drove by our house now and then to keep an eye on us. I would sit on the front porch and watch the cars pass and look for a familiar face in every window. When a plane would fly overhead, I would pretend it was my father checking to see if we were doing okay. Someday, when he got up the courage, he would have that pilot land on the roof of the laundromat across the street, and he’d say hello.

Years later, after I had my own kids, I thought he might be watching them, too. Had he read Sam's birth announcement in the paper, by chance? Doubtful, since he didn't know where I lived. (Or did he?) And how about the middle-aged man in working clothes at the grocery store who glanced too long at us while I picked through the produce? I thought it might be him, and I held an apple up to my son: "See the apple, honey? *La manzana, en español.*" I was showing off. The fact that this man couldn't possibly be my father posed no problem to my magical thinking. Maybe it was a friend of his. The wonderful, sensitive man was getting reports from his *friend*. Of course.

I wanted a dad who was clever and shy and wounded, so he was. I remember a study from a college psychology class, about how grieving survivors often think the person they've lost watches them from above, a guardian angel of sorts. Another study found that "children who experience the death of a parent exhibit problems similar to those of children who lose a parent through divorce." And then the punch line, buried in a footnote: when one divorced parent is "suddenly and consistently absent" (check), the child is worse off than if the parent had died.

I was about seven the only time he invited us to go on vacation. As we waited for him to pick us up, I wanted to back out. Would I be funny and smart enough? What might I do—a tap dance, jumping jacks, a witty response, a wise observation—to make him like me?

Finally, his green Ford lumbered into the driveway. I watched through a crack in the curtains as he made his way to the front door.

He spoke to Mom with a warm voice: “Am I taking these three rascals all the way to Arizona?” He wrote a check, the first and only, one leg propped on the kitchen chair, checkbook on his knee. He tore the check—*zzzt*—and handed it over in silence.

I stared while he spoke. His hair was curly and uncut. A shaggy mustache covered his upper lip, and his voice, when he summoned us to his car, was much softer than our stepfather’s.

The inside of his car smelled of dashboard dust and Camel cigarettes. Thirty years later I still remember that scent. We traveled in silence, eventually reaching the steep mountain slopes outside Tempe, Arizona, where his mother lived. And I thought, *This is what it feels like to go on vacation with your real father.*

Our drive began to seem long, and the twisting mountain roads scared me. The metal guard rails didn’t appear to offer much protection from a fall. My lap belt was half stuck in the crease of the seat, along with some loose tobacco the color of my dad’s hair. He wasn’t good at making conversation, which I took personally. As the road began to snake more severely, he slowed down, and other cars overtook us from behind. Going uphill, the old Ford’s engine sounded as if it didn’t want to be there.

He took us to a zoo, and out for pizza, and to the movies. He was more spectator than participant in everything we did. I felt vaguely like a character in a Dick and Jane book: *See the daughter. See her run. She is happy when she runs. The daughter likes to feed the birds. She laughs when she feeds the birds.* But I liked being some man's daughter just fine, and this father smiled often. He watched us watch the monkeys. He watched us eat our pizza. He watched me walk through the parking lot of the pizza place holding my red balloon. When the balloon popped unexpectedly, he dropped to the ground. We laughed, but he didn't.

That night he drank enough for me to make tall towers with the empty beer cans. We sat side by side in front of the blue glow of the television in my grandmother's trailer, watching *Apocalypse Now!* While everyone slept, my dad told me about a place called Vietnam. He talked of jungles that were wet and dense, and of horrors I couldn't fully comprehend. He spoke of children fleeing from helicopters that flew so close to the ground he could see their terrified faces as they ran. We did not make eye contact, but I felt special sitting beside him, my knees tucked inside my pajamas, his soft voice telling me grave and important things.

At the end of the week he brought us home. The car ride back was a little less quiet, the cigarette smoke a little heavier in my lungs. A block before we got to our house, he pulled over, put the car in park, and faced us. "Is he treating you good?" he asked, about our stepfather, Al.

Not really, I wanted to say. Yes, he could be loving, but he also called us names and yelled so loud that spit gathered in the corners of his mouth. And sometimes he pushed us, and other times he used his belt. "Do. You. Under. Stand?" A fit of rage, which ended in a hug.

My dad waited for my answer.

"Yes," I said. "He's nice to us."

He promised to call soon, and he waved as he drove away. I didn't see him again until his funeral.

My sisters and I were next of kin and therefore charged with settling his estate—which is to say, selling his car and emptying out his tiny apartment, one of many he'd lived in.

Did we find photos of our long-ago Arizona vacation in his closets? A withered cactus souvenir? No. There was not a trace of the ten days we'd spent together. None of the clothes we removed from his drawers looked familiar. There was no home movie footage of the zoo or our shiny young heads in the desert sun; no silent clips of us waving at the camera or clowning in the pool. There was no journal entry detailing the cost of our pizza that night in the mid-1970s, or his parking lot dive when the red balloon burst. If his apartment, which we'd never before seen, smelled of him, it didn't smell familiar.

The cause of death had not been hard to discern: He went to work in the morning, told a coworker he didn't feel well, turned gray, and died on the way to the emergency room. A heavy smoker, a red-meat eater, and an alcoholic, he'd had a heart attack at fifty-four, the same age his father had died. I saw a spatter of dried blood on the floor near the toilet in his bathroom. I don't know if it was related to his drinking or cow blood that he'd carried home from work at the packing plant. How startling, death, even when it makes sense. I'd spent a lifetime imagining reunions that I now knew would never happen.

My paternal grandmother was not much of an informant. Over the years after I'd moved back to Iowa, we'd established a routine: Every summer she would visit her sister's place in Sioux City, right up the road from the house where I'd lived when I was in high school, and my sisters Marie and Kathleen and I would stop by for an hour to see her. She'd bake her famous chocolate cake and homemade Twin Bing candy bars; we'd eat both. Then she'd stare wistfully at our faces while we pretended not to be uncomfortable. She would tell us over and over about the time my sister, at the age of three, had caught Grandpa eating in the living room, and she'd stomped her foot, yelled, and pointed, "In the kitchen!" Or my infant colic: "Good God, the way you cried!"

These were our grandmother's memories, not ours—select moments she chose. She never told us about the time she had to bail our father out of jail because our mom had refused to do it again. In the midst of a short annual visit, there was no good opportunity to bring up words like *abandonment, deadbeat,* or *alcoholic.* Instead we joked and chatted and asked polite questions. After posing for our yearly picture on the couch, hands full of leftover brownies, we'd hug goodbye until the following summer, when we'd relive "In the *kitchen*!" once more and hear Grandma's lovely, hacking smoker's laugh.

Clearing out my fifty-four-year-old dad's apartment alongside Grandma felt similar to one of those summer visits—minus the brownies, plus an air of devastation. The moment never felt right to ask difficult questions. Such discussions take time and courage, both of which we lacked. I wondered often whether he ever thought of us. Did he even acknowledge three daughters? My grandmother's refrain was "Tommy really loved you girls." I had no good response. We stuck to easy topics. Finding golf clubs, we asked, "Was he any good?" Every innocent question was an implication: Our father was a stranger to us. Grandma offered nothing concrete in response. Coming across his newly unwrapped Christmas presents—shirts and khaki pants from Macy's that she'd bought and sent only a week before—she extended them eagerly to our husbands. Nothing fit.

My friend Gina and I have a pact: Should either of us die unexpectedly, the other will retrieve the shoebox of sex toys hidden in the deceased's closet. Gina, in particular, wants to spare her mom, who doesn't believe in French kissing, from discovering her vibrator.

We all have secrets we want to keep from those who will survive us, maybe because we don't want to hurt them. Though, let's face it, what we want to spare them from is probably not what would pain them the most.

I was certainly prepared for the possibility of uncovering secrets when I emptied out my dad's apartment. Needles. Unpaid bills. Nasty letters. Corpses in freezers. Any of these would be rough discoveries, but that's not what I found.

Discovery One

Immediately after I walked into his apartment for the first time, one of my sisters handed me a framed eight-by-ten picture of the three of us. "Look what he had in his room," she said. It was the same photo I'd slipped into his pocket at the funeral, only larger.

"How do you know it was his?" I asked.

"Grandma found it on his TV, in the bedroom."

I didn't believe her.

I walked to the back of the apartment. The TV was in the center of the wall, facing his bed. Was our grandmother lying to make us feel good? I looked atop the TV and saw a clean, narrow strip in the dust where the frame had sat.

"It's a nice room," I said.

My sisters smiled, and my grandmother nodded with conviction. The mood was one of tiny celebration. Proof. Sweet, pathetic proof.

Discovery Two

He ate lots of mayo, white bread, and Pepsi. No sweets. Not surprisingly he also had a freezer full of red meat—mostly steaks. Also not a shock: the shelves packed with beer.

He had two George Foreman grills, one badly worn, the other brand-new and still in the box. Something about that made me deeply sad. I pictured him throwing a single burger on the grill night after night, wearing out the grill, and finally buying himself a new one—then dying before he opened the box.

Discovery Three

There was a woman at the funeral who didn't introduce herself or stay to talk. I didn't realize she was my dad's girlfriend until a week later, when I overheard my grandmother and aunt discussing her. This woman was the one who'd sent a plant addressed to "Tommy's family, with condolences," the one who'd left her pajamas at his apartment. I often wonder what was going through her mind at the funeral. I didn't see her cry.

Discovery Four

He did not appear to be a materialistic man, but he had a hell of a TV. The recliner in front of it held a pillow and a blanket, and the TV cabinet housed six long rows of movies, reaching from one wall to the next. Could this have been every war movie ever made? *To Hell and Back. The Longest Day. When Trumpets Fade. Saving Private Ryan. We Dive at Dawn. Strike Commando.* What was a *wonderful, sensitive* man doing watching all this violence?

I'd become a pacifist partly in response to my dad's post-traumatic stress disorder. I took my kids to anti-war rallies in slings and strollers before they could walk. This was my best attempt at saving them from my father's fate. Every time I demonstrated, I felt my father was with me in spirit. If we'd lived near each other, I assumed, he would have been there in person. After all, we both knew war turned kind men into absent fathers, didn't we? When fathers never saw their kids—that was because of war. He was a victim, my father: a working-class kid, not privileged enough to hide in the bunker of college or law school; a boy who got suckered by a nation willing to send its less advantaged kids to fight. We were a broken family because of my parents' divorce, and my parents' divorce was because of alcohol and trauma, and the alcohol and trauma were because of the Marines and Agent Orange and blasts in Vietnam. He despised all of that, didn't he?

As I ran my hands over his movie collection, the United States was puffing its chest, preparing for what would become Operation Iraqi Freedom. When the inevitable bright blasts resounded in the dark Iraqi sky, I imagined, it would be young men like my dad—doe-eyed, deep-dimpled boys with guns—who tramped off to war. I pictured him in a recliner, his face lit by the flickering glow of bomb blasts on the evening news, turning off the TV because it was too painful to watch.

And then my grandmother told me, *hell no, he wasn't disturbed by the buildup to war.* In fact, she said, "Tommy told me if we went to war, he'd go in a second. Except he said they might not want him—he was probably too damn old."

Discovery Five

He had a lifelong zeal for baseball, evidenced by a picture of him as a child in a ball cap, holding his bat and grinning. He had played his entire life, which explained the dirty cleats and uniforms, the weathered mitts and caps we found in his closet. His buddy Lenny told us after the funeral that Dad could have played in the Major Leagues. He said our dad had been clocked throwing a ninety-mile-per-hour fastball. I have no idea if this is true or just a well-intentioned brag, but I clung to it as my sons' rightful inheritance.

"Ninety miles per hour?" I said to B. that night in the hotel bed, as we were falling asleep. "Does that seem right?"

Discovery Six

He had an old Christmas tree and some ornaments that he never put up. His Marine dress blues hung in his closet. He had a stepson from a previous marriage. I'd known this last part. He'd been married to the boy's mother for about five years when she'd died in a car accident, pregnant with what would have been my father's fourth child. After that, the son went to live with his biological father and likely never saw my dad again.

Every picture he owned filled one manila envelope, including the few we'd sent to our grandmother over the years, which she had forwarded to him. There were many photos of him that seemed to have been taken at work. One featured an enormous birthday cake with a caricature of him on it, his bushy hair exaggerated to cartoonish proportions. In the photo he is standing beside the cake in his white coat and hairnet, his smile radiant, his dimples deep. I like this one because it means his coworkers knew his birthday and went to the trouble of buying a cake to celebrate. And he appeared to love it.

Discovery Seven

Porn. Conventional. Under the mattress.

Discovery Eight

Over potato salad and ham the day after the funeral, my dad's buddy Lenny was reminiscing with my grandmother about how "Tommy loved to gamble." She tried to change the subject. I wondered: How did Lenny know my grandmother so well? Lenny and my dad lived in Texas, while she lived in Arizona. I looked back and forth between her and Lenny, confused. Hadn't she just met him at the funeral like us?

Then Lenny said something about all the fun they'd had on their road trips to "the Belle." He teased Grandma about the way she yanked the slots with one arm and smoked with the other. I remembered my grandmother's summer visits to Iowa, and I asked if he meant the Belle of Sioux City, a riverboat-gambling casino I'd snuck into as a teen. "Yes," Lenny said, enjoying himself, "*that* Belle." My dad and my grandmother and Lenny went there for blackjack and bad buffet food every summer while Grandma was in Sioux City.

Every summer? My father stayed in the same house as my grandmother, a five-minute walk from mine, *every summer*? Not once did he stop by or call. Not once did I see a Ford with Texas plates drive by my house. (Believe me, I looked for those.) I wanted to put my fingers in my ears and rock back and forth: *Nah, nah, nah, nah. I can't hear you.*

This is the secret my dad should have kept hidden. He should have made a pact with Lenny to stuff this one deep into a closet and never let it see the light of day. He was supposed to be toiling in a meatpacking plant in Texas, sad and drunk and lonely, not taking road trips with his buddy—especially not road trips that ended four blocks from my house. Could he possibly have been such a callous man? Was my wonderful, sensitive, funny, wounded, absent father actually a selfish jerk?

I realize now how ludicrous it must seem that I was so surprised. After all, he never showed up for my life. But even as I write this, I try to rationalize: Maybe just being in proximity to my sisters and me was some comfort to him. Maybe he took the trip to Iowa to feel close to us without the risk of rejection, awkwardness, and pain. (Have I mentioned he was sensitive?)

Does it matter, really, what his reasons were?

Discovery Nine

A Thai family at his funeral kept smiling at me: a mother, a father, and a daughter. They approached me after the service with reverence.

"Did you know my dad?" I asked.

"Tommy liked our pepper steak," the man told me.

His daughter explained that he drove an hour every Friday night, from Childress to Amarillo, to eat in their family-run restaurant. His favorite meal was their pepper steak, and they made piles of it for him. He was more than a customer; he'd become a friend. They'd fed him in their home, compared grandchildren over dinner. He had mentioned my sister's daughter by name: *Mackenzie*. These strangers knew my niece's name.

"Was he happy?" I asked the family. Asking this aloud was the hardest thing I'd done so far, and I felt nauseated waiting for the answer. What if they said he wasn't? What if they said he was?

The man, woman, and daughter looked at each other. The father spoke Thai. The daughter translated.

"He was very happy to get a new girlfriend," she said warmly. "He thought he might have a wife and family sometime." She leaned toward me and touched my arm. "He felt happy for that. Hoping."

My sisters and I finished clearing out the tiny apartment, selling most of the contents to an auctioneer for two hundred dollars. I took his unopened George Foreman grill but never could bring myself to use it. Marie took his Marine uniform but has never removed it from the box. Kathleen took his battered baseball mitt and put it on her dresser.

A few years later, after the burial, after another move, Sam began to talk about the "man in the corner."

"What man, honey?" I said. "Where?"

He was in the corner of my bedroom, according to Sam, and he had wild hair. Maybe he was finally responding after years of imagined conversations. Maybe he was showing up, belatedly, which isn't the worst way to talk to the living and sure beats silence. Sam told me he mostly just smiled and said hello.

"Ah," I replied. I looked but saw nothing. "He's probably a nice man," I said, "just watching to see how we're doing."

FWD

From: jenny@talktome.com
Subject: Talking With You
Date: June 1, 2008 8:34 PM EST
To: dara@workwork.com

Dear Aunt D,

Can we find a good time to connect soon? I'd like to ask you a few questions about my dad. The older I get the more I wonder. Sam asked the other day at sunrise, "Did your dad have a loud voice or a mean voice?" I told him I wasn't sure, but possibly a gentle one. Did you have much contact with him before he died? I figure, hey—you're his sister. Any information you can give me is more than I have.

Look forward to talking with you soon.

From: dara@workwork.com
Subject: FWD: FWD: FWD: National GIRLFRIEND Week!
Date: June 2, 2008 9:20 AM MST
To: jenny@talktome.com, divabooty@aol.com, jaja@cyberbuddy.com 39 more...

To the cool women who have touched my life--here's to you! If you get this twice you know you have more than one girlfriend. I am only as strong as the coffee I drink, the hairspray I use, and the friends I have. It is good to be a woman:

1. We got off the Titanic first.
2. We don't have to pass gas to amuse ourselves.
3. We can talk to the opposite sex without having to picture them naked.
4. There are times when chocolate really can solve ALL your problems.
5. We can make comments about how silly men are in their presence because they aren't listening anyway.
6. Send this to all the bright women you know and make their day!!!!! LOVE YA! Mean it!

From: jenny@talktome.com
Subject: Still wanting to connect
Date: August 18, 2008 8:10 PM EST
To: dara@workwork.com

Aunt Dara!

You must be pretty busy. No one ever answers at your place. Could you email me the best times to reach you? Or feel free to call my number anytime.

Hey, the Cubs are looking good this season! I bet Dad would've been thrilled. He was a lifelong fan, right? (My mother says yes, but her memory is suspect.) I almost hope they don't make it to the World Series. How heartbreaking for it to finally happen after he's died. He would've been 55 this year; today, in fact, is his birthday, no?

I'd love to talk to you soon.

From: dara@workwork.com
Subject: FWD: FWD: FWD: Blonde Logic!
Date: August 19, 2008 6:37 AM MST
To: jenny@talktome.com, divabooty@aol.com, jaja@cyberbuddy.com 39 more...

BLONDE LOGIC

IN A VACUUM

A blonde was playing Trivial Pursuit one night. It was her turn. She rolled the dice and she landed on Science & Nature. Her question was, "If you are in a vacuum and someone calls your name, can you hear it?"

She thought for a time and then asked, "Is the vacuum on or off?"

SEND TO TEN SOMEONES WHO COULD USE A LAUGH. NOW GO!!! ☺

From: jenny@talktome.com
Subject: Questions for you
Date: October 19, 2008 9:39 AM EST
To: dara@workwork.com

Aunt Dara,

It appears you're on email often, so hopefully you'll have a second to read and respond to this. You do know my sisters and I didn't know our dad, right?

What kind of man was he? Did he talk about us?

Was he happy?

I realize you and I don't really know each other, but you are my dad's sister, a warm-blooded link to the dead who shares his gold-flecked blue eyes and possibly some treasured insight. I would love to hear from you.

Your niece,

Jenny

From: dara@workwork.com
Subject: FWD: FWD: FWD: [FWD]: [FWD]: You're special light
Date: October 20, 2008 7:21 AM MST
To: jenny@talktome.com, divabooty@aol.com, jaja@cyberbuddy.com 39 more...

When life hands you lemons, ask for tequila and salt and call me over!!!

Life should NOT be a journey to the grave with the intention of arriving safely in an attractive and well preserved body, but rather to skid in sideways, chocolate in one hand, wine in the other, body thoroughly used up, totally worn out and screaming 'WOO HOO what a ride!'

Have a wonderful day!

KEEP THE HAND OF FRIENDSHIP GOING! SEND TO SOMEONE WHO NEEDS A WAVE!!!

PS: Happy International Very Good Looking Damn Smart Women's Day.

From: jenny@talktome.com
Subject: ME AGAIN!
Date: October 23, 2008 11:59 PM EST
To: dara@workwork.com

Aunt Dara,

I spoke with my mother. She said my father wrote letters from Vietnam? She thinks he sent many to you. Is that true? If so, I can't tell you what it would mean to me to be able to read them. I've never seen his handwriting. Was he more intimate on the page than in person?

Would you send them to me?

If you don't want to give up the letters, I'll reimburse you for copies.

Thank you.

Jenny

From: dara@workwork.com
Subject: FWD: FWD: FWD]: Angel of faith
Date: October 27, 2008 8:12 PM MST
To: jenny@talktome.com, divabooty@aol.com, jaja@cyberbuddy.com <u>39 more</u>...

Worry looks around, Sorry looks back, Faith looks up.

This angel is sent to protect you. **BUT FIRST: You must send her to 8 people including me.** In 8 minutes you will receive something you have long awaited. Have Faith.

From: jenny@talktome.com
Subject: Re: FWD: Angel of faith
Date: October 28, 2008 6:04 AM EST
To: dara@workwork.com, onevictim@net.net, twovictim@net.net 5 more...

Hey hey! Back at ya! Just like you asked—8 people including *you*. I know you're not supposed to tell wishes, but I wished for those letters.

-----FWD. FWD
From: dara@workwork.com
Subject: FWD: FWD: FWD]: Angel of faith
Date: October 27, 2008 8:12 PM MST
To: jenny@talktome.com, divabooty@aol.com, jaja@cyberbuddy.com 39 more...

Worry looks around, Sorry looks back, Faith looks up.

This angel is sent to protect you. BUT FIRST: You must send her to 8 people including me. In 8 minutes you will receive something you have long awaited. Have Faith.

From: dara@workwork.com
Subject: FWD: FWD: [FWD]: Hear Our PRAYERS
Date: October 24, 2008 8:33 AM MST
To: jenny@talktome.com, divabooty@aol.com, jaja@cyberbuddy.com 39 more...

Please God hear this, my prayer: If you can't make me thin make my girlfriends fat.

From: jenny@talktome.com
Subject: FWD: Wildly Popular Email Questionnaire
Date: November 1, 2008 6:31 AM EST
To: dara@workwork.com

Hey all! I don't usually forward these things but this *widely disseminated* email looked kinda fun. **IMPORTANT**: Answer *every* question or you won't get the prize at the end. BE HONEST.

1. What are you doing *right* now?
2. Did you ever serve in Vietnam?
3. Did your brother?
4. What's your favorite cookie?
5. What was your brother's favorite cookie?
6. Do you know anyone who abandoned three young daughters then died of a heart attack before they were reunited?
7. If *yes* to #6 above, why did he do that?
8. Did this person ever get arrested? If yes, can you please say why?
9. CATCH THIS: If you live in the MIDWEST, make this paragraph about anyone with brown hair. If you live in NY, make it about someone who is younger than you. If your name starts with a 'D' and you live in Wyoming this paragraph must be about . . . **your BROTHER!**

DO THIS. THEN SEND IT TO EVERYONE IN YOUR ADDRESS BOOK OR YOUR PUP WILL SUFFER A TERRIBLE FATE. ☺ ☺ ☺ Now GO!!!

BONUS: IF you have written correspondence from the person you wrote about in question #9 and that person is deceased and you send his correspondence via snail mail to just ONE interested party you could win one million dollars.

From: dara@workwork.com
Subject: FWD: FWD: FWD: FWD: FWD: FAMILY MATTERS
Date: November 2, 2008 9:20 AM MST
To: jenny@talktome.com, divabooty@aol.com, jaja@cyberbuddy.com 39 more…

When we began this adventure called womanhood, we had no idea of the incredible joys or sorrows that lay ahead. Nor did we know how much we would need each other.

Every day, we need each other still.

Pass this gift of flowers on to all the women who help make your life meaningful. I just did. Short and so sweet.

From: jenny@talktome.com
Subject: Am I HEARING YOU CORRECTLY?
Date: November 2, 2008 1:43 PM EST
To: dara@workwork.com

Dear Aunt Dara,

I've been thinking a lot about everything you've said lately. Sometimes over email it's hard to know what you mean.

What you're trying to say, I guess, is:

Recipes are like a dating service. They never end up looking like the picture. There should be a support group for women who can't put their dishes in the dishwasher dirty. I love a good meal so I don't cook. The only thing I stir up in the kitchen is trouble. If it fits in a toaster I can cook it.

Now you're cookin'!

Chocolate is a food group. I break for candy.

When you have to walk that lonesome valley and you have to walk it by yourself, the women in your life will be on the valley's rim, cheering you on. Sisters are there, no matter how many miles are between you. A girlfriend is never farther away than needing her can reach.

There are more than twenty angels in this world. Ten are peacefully sleeping on clouds. Nine are playing. And one is reading her email at this moment. Is it you? No, it's me.

Be somebody's angel.

Love is your sister shopping with you the day after Thanksgiving. Love is letting your best friend borrow your thong.

Life's too short to pass on love.

Save a life; send this to everyone you know.

From: dara@workwork.com
Subject: FWD: FWD: Bridges 'tween Friends.
Date: November 3, 2008 8:01 AM MST
To: jenny@talktome.com, divabooty@aol.com, jaja@cyberbuddy.com 39 more...

We is friends! Me and you is friends.
You smile, I smile.
You hurt, I hurt.
You cry, I cry.
You jump off a bridge, I gonna miss your emails.

Don't break this; it's really working!!!!!!

An Inquiry into Epigenetics

epi:
On top of, (or in addition to) . . . genetics

epi:
On top of, like a padlock, clasped around our DNA, until something—(a toxin, good love, a war)—flicks it open. Epigenetics isn't the study of the DNA; it's the study of the lock and the key.

genetics:
Before I was born, my father sent his mother a letter from Vietnam. It said:

> Those jets take off all night long while I'm trying to sleep.
> We're right in Danang right near the airstrip, so it sounds like they are coming through our little house.
> Those supersonic jets are really loud.

My son runs to my room at all hours of the night. He has since he could walk. The ghosts follow him, sometimes ethereal, more often wrapped like mummies.

The scientists are saying: Epigenetics has proven that changes in gene expression are passed down to our offspring for at least one generation. Epigenetics can't decide which chromosomes go to your baby or your grandbaby, but it can decide which chromosomes wake up and express themselves, which get to speak the hell up and which have to shush.

My father's letters also said:

> We've had rifle classes, pistol classes, Marine Corp history classes, guidance classes, interior guard classes, government classes, and first aid classes. We've had 6 hours of hand-to-hand combat classes and 3 hours of bayonet classes.

Many years I've researched my father's war. Many years I've worried about Sam's ghosts.

And his letter said:

> Oh, that cake you sent me didn't look too much like a cake when I got it. I wasn't here more than a couple hours and I had an M-14 and 20 rounds. (Now I have to go because this is my last sheet of paper.)

We built that core narrative early: the pizza, the parking lot, *the red balloon pop.* His duck-and-cover. When he dropped beside us in that parking lot he was also, in that moment, eighteen in a jungle. That kid's flinching, wound inside his own kids' genes and theirs.

Neurobiologists have bred fear into mice. They take male mice and fill the air with acetophenone, a chemical that smells like cherries. Each time the room fills with the smell of cherries, they administer small electric shocks to the mice. When those same mice are later exposed to acetophenone without shock, they "shudder" and show other signs of fear. The scared mice go on to father pups that shudder when exposed to acetophenone, despite not once being shocked themselves. That generation of mice, too, fathers pups that shudder when exposed to the sweet smell of cherries, despite never being shocked.

When I was sixteen I wrote my first term paper. I stumbled upon a topic called *post-traumatic stress disorder.* Soldiers from Vietnam, I learned, did not take the long, slow boat home but instead were plucked from the jungle one day, and dropped into their childhood bedrooms the next.

So mice can inherit PTSD triggered by the smell of cherries. Some scientists call this a breakthrough. Others call it bogus, because, what's the mechanism? *Find me,* they say, *your demyelinated cherry-leery, scaredy-cat-chromosome and place it in my disbelieving hand.*

My son, at age two, pointed at a military airplane in the overcast Michigan sky and his whole body shook. Though we never knew why, he called that plane and all others, "ah bomb."

A graduate school classmate of mine once read an essay about my father and said an alcoholic Vietnam vet who abandons his children, has trouble with the law, and dies unhappy seems awfully cliché. I should change the story, she said, if I possibly could.

I agreed.

When the drumbeats sounded in protest against the war in Iraq, I brought my son to protests. He bounced up and down to the rhythm of a protester's bongos and held a cardboard sign that said, "No War!"

At the age of four, Sam said to me:
In my dream, the ghosts come into my body to decide if I am alive or dead. They are too cold.

Haunting, I realize, does not distinguish between the physical or the imagined, the literal or the metaphorical. Haunted expresses itself as haunted.

My sister-in-law wrote songs to honor my son's nascent vocabulary. The Airplane Song went like this: "Wait! What's that thing over there? Flying high in the sky over there? It's ah bomb! It's ah bomb! It's ah bomb, bomb, bomb bomb bomb!"

There's a photo of my son on our wall. He's wearing denim overalls and tiny shoes and holding the pint-sized-sign that says, "No War!" Call it sweet or crazy or sad; I call it proof: this boy was raised to opt out. Legally, I believe we'd call him a *conscientious objector.*

For years, I thought my father rode in a helicopter that dropped napalm. Now I can't confirm whether that's true or a story my young mind made up to explain his absence. Either way and because of stories told on that red-balloon night, I've pictured Kim Phuc, the naked girl, running injured, while my father hovered inches above her. I imagined he didn't want to be there, doing that, but he did anyway, and I imagined he saw the faces of the villagers who fled.

My boy's thoughts are blisters, tender for his mind to touch.

A psychoanalyst who studied trust vs. mistrust, intimacy vs. isolation, "the hazards of existence" (and militant nonviolence), explains the potential paradox of the *epigenetic principle*: "Anything that grows has a ground plan, and that out of this ground plan, the parts arise, each part having its time of special ascendancy . . . until all parts have arisen to form a functioning whole." The question: What *whole* does our body build toward? And what influences or interrupts it along the way?

I reach out to a Marine named Dave who fought on Monkey Mountain the same time as my father. He doesn't recall ever meeting my dad, but he's confirmed they were in the same place at the same time. Offering himself as a proxy, he shares memories. In an email loaded with photos he explains,

"Here's a shot of naval gunfire hitting targets south of us . . . A couple of night shots of the air base getting hit during the Tet Offensive . . . A few shots of a Navy jet that crashed on the edge of our road. Nothing too graphic, just the stuff we would send home to Mama or our sweethearts."

Fresh from the jungle and asleep in his childhood bed, my father woke to his little sister, pouncing on him by way of hello. He bolted upright, grabbed a letter opener, and aimed it at her throat.

The students and I read *The Things They Carried*. We read about dog tags and cigarettes and heat tabs, and we talk about the literal things the men in Vietnam carried. We talk about how Jimmy Cross humped his love for Martha up the hills. Then the men write about people they love by listing the things they carry. I learn about the insides of a mother's purse and a brother's coat pocket and a war buddy's field notebook. One man describes a jail key he once carried in his pocket, rubbing it when he felt tempted to go astray to remind him he never wanted return to prison.

My father has been to jail and my father has been in Vietnam. It surprises me when I realize I have no idea what he carried.

I do know what he left behind.

For my birthday I pay a psychic to contact my father's ghost, but I'm not sure he shows up. I want to confirm my years-ago suspicion that he did not stick around because PTSD wouldn't allow it. Instead, the psychic only smiles and she says: "You're the apple of his eye. He's pointing at his eye and saying you're the apple."

Research doesn't know about any apple in the eye, but it has plenty to say about anxious parents. Scientist Michael Kobor finds a parent's anxiety "leads to discernable changes in [the offspring's] 'epigenome,' measurable more than a decade later. This literally provides a mechanism by which experiences get under the skin."

When Sam was a baby he cried for six months straight. I'd pat his back and rock him and tell him the most comforting thing I could think to say: *I know, I know.*

A human narrative woven with genetics and war. Is this a new story or the oldest? A kid took a trip from Sioux City, Iowa, to Monkey Mountain, where he was given an M14 and 20 rounds, where he heard supersonic jets and watched the sun rise for two years in the jungle. That kid did or did not lower a helicopter on villagers and watch them flee. He later came home, slaughtered cows for a living, had babies, and left babies. That kid's daughter gave birth to a butter-skinned, burnt sugar, sleep-light boy with restless legs. The two boys never met but they intersect in time and space. One kid stepped off the boat in 1967 Vietnam and each blast that resonated in his chest cavity vibrates—four decades and two generations later—inside a Lego-strewn room on a hill in Saint Paul that holds a red rug at the end of a bed, which belongs to a boy who runs from death day and night.

For one scientific second, let's blame epigenetics for our ghosts. For one scientific second, let's imagine my son was drafted before birth.

When Sam runs toward me like a man pursued, I make eye contact, and he pretends he's not afraid.

It sure was a funny feeling anchored off the coast last night, watching the flares going up and the lights all over on top of the hills.

The ghosts come into my body to decide if I am still alive or dead. They are so cold.

We're right in Danang right near the airstrip so it sounds like they are coming through our little house.

It's nighttime and I know that sound. I hear my son's feet slam against the floor, then run toward me. In bed at night, the unquiet part of my mind waits for the door to bang open, for my son's body to pass through.

Open Window, Burning House

1.

I HAD NO IDEA my dad had been locked up when I walked through the sally port to teach my first class at Lino Lakes Prison. Those sliding metal doors mark the liminal space between the known world and the hidden, between community and isolation. It's in this transitional zone where volunteers receive the UV stamp on our hands—invisible permission to enter, blacklight proof that we can leave. I'd experienced this routine, alongside others, for four years before ever learning my dad had run-ins with the law.

He disappeared from my life by choice, some thirty years before he messed up. The time he did do—a year in jail, not prison—was a blink in relation to the decades endured by many of the people I care about. I don't consider myself systems-impacted, unlike over two and a half million others in the United States. A cage was not to blame for my father's absence. But I know enough to realize my dad's arrests would've entitled him to a range of humiliations from cuffing to strip searching, and the raised-eye-religious-sanctimony of a Texas jail. I know it happened during the worst time in his life. I know it severed him from human connection exactly when he needed it most.

Once in a while I work with someone also severed from the world, who reminds me of him, or at least the man I imagine he was. Like the gray-haired grandfather in my narrative nonfiction class, who twisted his beard at the tip and mentioned his relatively minor charge every chance he got. Each time he recited his crime—something students rarely do—he seemed to be telling not the story of who he was, but the story of who he was not. Almost every class, he'd note his one-year sentence beside others who were serving decades. On the page he dodged his narrative like it was fatal. His stories stubbornly offered nothing: no character, no setting, no plot.

"What's your story telling us?" I asked him once after weeks of gently pressing for a *who* or a *what.*

"Just that some things went wrong. Like shit tends to." He looked angry at me in a way a student never had. "Make it whatever you want."

Who can blame him? Examining your life on the page can be exhausting. And to do so inside a system that assumes if you exist inside those walls, you deserve suspicion, condescension, and a requisite number of calories each day?

I paused, and before I could follow up, the writer beside him cleared his throat and said, "Actually, it's kinda like, it could be a trip to Hawaii."

And another man agreed: "Or could be an open window on a burning house. That's cool how he made it so it could be anything."

Around the table, people sensed his frustration. They shifted their comments accordingly.

Consensus was, yep: The story could be whatever the reader wants.

The guard called switch out, and the class packed up their books and left the room, shaking my hand before walking out of the building.

Except the man whose story could be anything. He left class that day and never came back.

* * *

It's not news that there are carceral systems that work differently than those in America, some better, some worse, by recidivism stats, or measures of common sense and compassion. My curiosity around how, why, and to what effect is the reason I traveled to Halden Fengsel, a maximum-security prison in Norway's far south.

The train ride to Halden curves along the Tista River, through endless rises of green, slowing in a town near the fortress on the hill, just a few miles from Sweden's border to the east. After my train sighs into the railway station, I walk to my hotel along a stretch of cobbled street. It's midday when I arrive, which means my hotel serves a snack of heart-shaped waffles. In the morning—salmon and cheese and fresh bread. A ceramic bowl in the hallway overflows with chocolates.

Norway gentles you into everything. And I wonder how that culture manifests in its prisons. Can beauty and kind touches markedly improve a horrible situation, or just mask a tough reality? Does "humane" take the edge off of "alone?" And if so, does that change the story we tell ourselves about ourselves?

Halden Fengsel, to my surprise, stands foreboding on approach, with twenty-foot concrete walls that blend into a gray sky. Its dystopian gates groan open, but once inside the building offers a different energy entirely: soft lights and forest views and quiet hellos. "Good cop, bad cop," manifest through architecture.

The warden smiles when he asks what I wish to see.

"What are my options?" I ask.

"Absolutely anything," he says, like he means it. "Whatever you want."

But first, I'm required to view a sit-down, hour-long, seventy-three-slide PowerPoint. On our way to the presentation, I pass walls covered in visual art, textiles, and poems, chosen by the staff, with the stated intention to be "in a humanistic tradition . . . to represent care without being preachy," in order to be "in dialogue with the inmates and staff." Art that's talking with people, in other words, not at them. A building in which living units look like IKEA showrooms, if IKEAs were built in the woods with floor-to-ceiling windows overlooking birch stands.

If a building can be said to nurture, this one tries hard, which is one of many reasons it's called the most humane maximum-security prison in the world. From amenities to interpersonal dynamics to light, this place invites folks, at minimum, to serve their time in relative sanity. Windows overlook a yard edged in trees, not concrete. And inside this building from which men cannot escape, folks wear their own clothes, not a uniform, and everyone greets one another. *Hei, heisan, hello.*

I wonder if it feels maddening to have your liberty removed in a place where people celebrate the incarcerators as enlightened, or if any attempt at kindness makes the global praise tolerable. I feel relieved, in any case, to be here as a writer where my curiosity is part of the contract. When I'm teaching, such curiosity feels misplaced at best, a betrayal at worst. I've known many of my students now for over a decade, and I see how hard they work to thrive in a system that works against wellness, to say nothing of survival. I don't ask about lockdowns or canceled visits, because that's not what they came to class to discuss, or what I came to talk about, either, but I see the destruction; it's impossible to ignore.

Here, questions aren't just appropriate, they're expected. Norway aims to transform their own systems, and to change the way the other countries practice incarceration. Per a white paper written to ensure more effective rehabilitation and a safer society, Norway asserts:

> Punishment is the restriction of liberty. No other rights are deprived from the inmate, i.e., he/she has the same rights as other habitants in Norway. No-one shall serve their sentence under stricter circumstances than necessary for the safety of the society. Life in prison shall resemble life in the community as much as possible.

Halden's warden, to his credit, shares context about the people they incarcerate, and that context implicates everyone. His PowerPoint titled "The Inmate: Who Is He?" tells any visitor to this prison:

> 60% had problems in upbringing (financially, housing, intoxication, abuse)
> 30% had contact with child welfare services before age 16
> 30% had family in jail
> 40% have only elementary school education
> 70% are unemployed
> 40% are below poverty line
> 30% have mental disorders
> 60% are substance abusers
> 50% have children

The presentation covers programming, and lots of it: from design and craftwork to communication and media graphics to information technology, photography, cooking, and woodworking. They favor integration over isolation—and as such, incorporate prison offerings like library access, education, and labor services into the very buildings where people live. Or, said differently, they house people inside a robust community.

After years of teaching in the US system, I can't help but wonder about the one thing Halden offers but doesn't talk about: religious programming. To study a prison's faith-based programming is to understand the sanctioned mythology about the humans they house; this mythology hints at the low bar—for perception and treatment of others—that the system itself will condone. The default rhetoric: *remorse, repent, atone,* all for the purpose of "offender change"—a Christian ethic, but minus mercy or shared culpability. The problem is harm does not happen in a vacuum, people are never just one thing, and prisons care nothing for mercy.

"When men come to prison," Halden's Chaplain Faanes tells me, "bad thoughts boil inside their heads, making them crazy." For that, Halden offers silent retreats modeled after Saint Ignatius's spiritual exercises. Saint Ignatius of Loyola was plain Inigo before he was canonized, a rich kid turned wounded soldier turned penitent, and his journey began the day he sat, alone and in silence, on the banks of the Cardoner River. Beside rushing water, the man who later became the author of *The Spiritual Exercises* and founder of the Jesuits, said of himself in third person: "The eyes of his understanding began to be opened. It was as if he were a new man." Instead of leaving the river and walking back up the hill to return to the posh life he knew, Inigo moved into a nearby cave where he prayed, fasted, and gave penance. His story is told with emphasis on that single moment at the river, where change overtook him like a seizure.

"Change, just like that?" I ask.

Chaplain Faanes thinks so.

He explains Halden doesn't have space for these silent retreats—no convent, no cave—so they kick everyone out of Unit C, lock it down, and kneel in silence, heads bowed, pens on the page, writing in journals.

The Spiritual Exercises are so emotionally taxing,

Chaplain Faanes tells me, that would-be penitents must go through months of preparation before they can even begin the retreat. The most difficult part of the preparation, he claims, is the silence—an inability to escape thoughts, feelings, the self. Like writing, I think. Halden participants can choose whether to continue, or to quit. If they choose the former, they'll withdraw from the daily routine of the prison and undergo a long internal journey meant to resemble the one Ignatius experienced in his cold cave.

"Silence is our *most important* tool," Chaplain Faanes stresses. He lowers his voice, crosses his feet. Inside silence, men move through four stages: white (goodness), red (love), black (sin and atonement), and blue (new choices, new life). The (atheist) writing teacher in me notes that Saint Ignatius asks participants to undergo a method of contemplation called "application of the senses." Ignatius felt evoking the senses developed the empathy needed to imitate God. Participants might, for instance, place themselves inside a scene from the Gospels and ask, "What do I see? What do I hear? What do I feel, taste, and smell?"

They might smell lamb roasting at the last supper.

They might hear the clatter of broken dishes during Christ's arrest.

If an introductory creative writing class follows any gospel, it's surely "application of the senses." In writing classes the world over, mine included, instructors ask students to place themselves inside the sensory, inside memory. Remember your childhood kitchen? What did the cooking sound like? Where did the light stream in? Where did the dog lay?

Did someone brown butter in a pan? Who did you wait for that never arrived? It can be emotionally taxing work, especially if the scenes from memory are painful. One writer I work with, V., says that when he writes memoir, he has to do so in bed, under a blanket, because the stories are too heavy for him to sit upright.

Maybe it's a similar weight that causes men to back out of the retreat. Chaplain Faanes emphasizes that yes, many back out, but when one stays, he learns to replace bad thoughts with better ones. At the end of three silent weeks many "forgive themselves and are forgiven."

Meh. I was with him till now.

Prior to meeting with the chaplain, I walked through a grocery store stocked with fresh fruit where incarcerated residents shop, a restaurant-quality kitchen where those same folks train to become chefs. All this to the backdrop of handshakes and warm conversation.

But just down the hall from organic apples and fancy stoves, what I'm hearing in Chaplain Faanes's office sounds like the same redemption narrative that's offered in US prisons.

I stare at him, hoping for more.

He looks at me like I just don't get it.

Right vs. wrong, broken vs. healed, ruined vs. redeemed. Even inside a softly lit building with art that is smart and texture on the walls, it's still a way of punishing a handful individuals for the problems of an entire society. It's still saying "change your criminal thinking," which is another way of saying "you are broken and in need of repair," not, mind you, "*we* are broken; we need repair."

I'm not trying to bust Norway, to say they're pretending at reform. Quite the opposite, really. It's telling in that context that religious programming—Prison-Christianity, especially—is conspicuously missing from their descriptions, descriptions that increasingly influence prison policy the world over.

"This is penance," Chaplain Faanes tells me flatly, pointing at the yard, the way one mansplains when he's bored. *Penance,* from the Latin *pænitentia*; related to *repentance,* from the Latin meaning to "cause or feel regret," or "is not enough," "is unsatisfactory." The root word *pen* means "punishment, pain."

2.

When I did discover my dad had been arrested many times, placed in county jail no fewer than four, he was already dead and I'd taught many fatherless fathers, men carrying blue-ink poems about Grandma's swollen ankles, a son's jelly-smeared smile turned indifferent grin. Their own words, not written in third person like Saint Ignatius inside his cave, but autobiographies, nonetheless. If the folks in my family who'd been locked up—dad, wayward grandpa, cousins—had been in my class over the years, they've might've written:

I liked to make my mother laugh.   When they came for me,
I wouldn't leave the closet. It's the only way I
could shut off my brain.   I had a 90 MPH fast-pitch unrealized,
underutilized: coulda played for the Majors.

I wanted to hurt myself; woke up blacked out had no idea how I got there. It was damn good money. I remember the light
in the hallway when I was eight; I was scared.
I didn't know what else to do
scared I crashed a car into a pole—and
it just rolled and rolled.

Poet Natalie Diaz writes, "I am. I am and am and am. What have I done?" Carceral systems ask people to wrestle with the question in the reverse: What have I done? I am. I am and am and am.

The sheriff who lorded over the system where my dad served his longest stint governed through shame. I remember feeling the insult in my stomach the first time I read that this sheriff, who I'll call Shitty Sheriff, used the word "maggot" to refer to the incarcerated in his jails, that he loved to evoke "Bubba," who waited for the newly convicted. Shitty Sheriff, like a cheesy B-rate movie actor, said: "Bingo! The maggot goes to jail. Right now he's having sunshine pumped to him. My bet is that somebody gets to spend a whole lot of time with our friend Bubba. Maybe the maggot can try and sucker-punch Bubba. That'd be fun to see."

Juvenile as that sounds, his rhetoric influenced an entire ecosystem, which impacted people; those people influenced the communities they returned to. Imagine that sort of deterioration to folks who do ten, fifteen, twenty years. Imagine that destruction increasing year after year, as connections with the outside world fray and snap.

After seeing the way the system needles at a man's identity, I wonder how even a short stay behind bars altered the way my dad viewed himself. I feel uncomfortable voicing this thought, let alone writing about it, because I know so many people who've done "real time." I tell this to a friend who works in the criminal legal system, and he grows serious. He tells me his sister was jailed for one weekend and it "fucked her up for years." The humiliation, he says, did more harm than the punishment did good.

My dad's arrest records include a series of mug shots taken over ten years, the first snapped when he was forty-two, the last taken a decade later, the year before his death. Prior to finding them, I'd seen only pictures from way back: a foggy black-and-white shot of a curly-haired kid in baseball pants, a grainy polaroid of a young father bending low to drink from a lion's mouth water fountain. His mug shots were among the only photos I'd seen of him as a middle-aged man, and as such, they double as daughter's flip-book. There he is, my dad—at my exact age!—with dense curls, a tan. In each shot, he ages. He is my dad exactly, of course, but changing before my eyes and under hard circumstances. Repeat, repeat, repeat, until the final photo, which was taken a year before he died, shortly after his last release.

* * *

Shitty Sheriff likely never read Seneca: *A man is as wretched as he has convinced himself he is.* Such a man, I'd argue, might conflate someone's worst act with their entire story.

An incarcerated friend of mine says you serve a life sentence regardless of how many years you live in prison because you will never shake the shame of doing time and no one on the outside will forget it either. You'll be entombed inside that narrative. Who needs Seneca or even abusive sheriffs when we live online—changing the world, one social media post at a time—ready to condemn and cancel without an ounce of context:

just eat pipes like the meth heads;   these men are
SCUMBAGS who deserve to be treated like it;
bullets are cheaper than court costs   garbage;
bang, bang, die; die;   for real, you people need jesus;

These are comments about men whose narrative was—at least partially—father, brother, potter, clerk, soldier, friend. Many of them caused harm. Many of them have been harmed. We know this.

Now what?

Retribution aside, *what next?*

Where is the space that reminds a man of his fast pitch, his guitar, his razor-sharp wit, the house he once painted for that neighbor, the song he sang to his niece at three a.m.? What would it look like if our response to harm made a person's most luminous storylines more visible, not invalid?

* * *

Reminded is the word my students use time and again when they talk about transformation. They say, writing reminded me I was smart. Class reminded me who I used to be. More times than I can count students have said to me: I *remember* what it feels like to care about something.

They teach me, year after year, that *transformation* is a reunion with the best parts of the self. A bumping into brightness that has always existed.

3.

Shitty Sheriff went to jail for corruption. He sold county services to the highest bidder. For those in his custody, he bought the worst-quality food. For himself, he bought yacht voyages to sunny places. Yes, he stole, and it's the monetary theft that landed him in a cell beside the men he called maggots, though it's the less visible theft—scything the stories of those in his care—that's arguably more damaging to our community, and which the system encouraged all along.

There's a webpage for the sheriffs of my dad's county. It's a photographic record of all twenty-five (white, male) sheriffs dating back to 1889. Beneath Shitty Sheriff's suit-and-tie photo is a banner that says *Removed from Office*.

My glee at seeing that makes me a hypocrite. How quickly my values change when it impacts one of my own. Which is why, Norway insists, we need policies and practices that are more humane than our personal response to hurt. In order to soften the bitter edge with Shitty Sheriff, I try to imagine his childhood—the narrative lens through which I meet most of my students. I picture Baby Shitty Sheriff in footie pj's held by a mom frying eggs in bacon grease in a steamy kitchen, and even still, I struggle to break through to caring. When that doesn't work, I imagine the damage years of isolation will do to this already-unwell person and I know spending time—especially in his own prisons, with the culture he fostered—worsens everything. Is it markedly better somewhere like Norway, where community is fostered and peer pressure demands more complex stories? If Halden were a man and that man were your cellie, he'd for sure offer a cigarette, even if he waited for you to confess to your brokenness as he held out a beautiful, hand-crafted ashtray. And when you ashed in his art, he'd at least make eye contact while he was judging, only a little, and less narrowly than America. When you were done, he'd offer you real food. I wish, in the midst of the indignities before, during, or even after my dad's unraveling (or anyone's), someone had invited him to write a poem about his childhood kitchen or the things he himself carried.

I have no idea how my dad would've told his own story if he'd been invited to. Allow me to try on his behalf? His mother stocked the kitchen with his favorites—chocolate cake and bologna sandwiches—because she loved to spoil him, most of all of her four children. His dad drove a fork-lift, his mom waited tables, and the six of them lived in eight hundred square feet. When he turned eighteen, his country tossed a gun his way and shipped him to the jungle. He came home. He self-medicated. For years, his beloveds bailed him out of trouble. When I was very young, he moved us as a family, away from family, and he never went back.

Somewhere in here I knew him, though I remember him in my cells more than my mind. Somewhere I gained the foggy sense of someone clever, mischievous, and smart. An introvert, a tender-heart, an addict, he must have felt the push-pull of retreating while needing others; I suspect this because it's in my blood, too. Long after he'd given up knowing his daughters, his second wife died in a car accident while pregnant with the baby who would've been his only son. That was the year of the first mug shot, when the man in the photo still looks young. Many mug shots later we reunited at his funeral—shortly after he'd been released from jail, no visitors, no mail.

Those are some of the only photos I have of his later years. I'd have preferred the flip-book that didn't materialize: selfies of him smoking at a kitchen table, my two sons on his lap, my sisters in the background, his eyes staring into the camera. Wrinkles deepen. His hair grays. His grandchildren, once crawling on the floor, now beside him, hands on his arm. They age in his kitchen, my dad and our children, over decades of dinners. Repeat, repeat, repeat, until the final photo, which is taken when he's ninety. His family—daughters, grandkids—at the same table where we've eaten years of meals. He looks tired, but also content.

That story wasn't so out of reach.

I like to imagine when my dad was at his lowest point in life—just after his wife and son died—someone would've invited him to share a memory, a cigarette, his favorite song, a poem. Not just because that makes sense, but because he was in pain, and because he was my dad.

I don't mean to excavate or mythologize my father or my students. I don't mean drag into the light stories that wish to stay in the dark. I just wonder about him. I wonder if he felt alone. I wonder what hurt him, and what would've helped.

My father's story: some things went wrong like shit tends to do.

No, it's kinda like a trip to Hawaii, an open window on a burning house.

That's cool how we do that.

Candling Delicious

For the first: P., K., D., M., J., and L.

To be alive, actually existing, to have emerged from darkness and silence, to be here to-day is certainly incredible.

—W. MACNEILE DIXON

1.

ON THE DESK IN my living room, beside the telephone and above the school directory, sits a makeshift incubator. It's a Styrofoam cooler impaled on one side by a work light; its venting system is comprised of puncture holes covered in duct tape as the temperature demands. The top of the incubator has a window made of plexiglass, through which you see a dozen chicken eggs that will hatch exactly twenty-one days post-incubation. Sam, who wants to be a street artist when he grows up, sketched a farm scene across the front of the cooler. The picture shows two red barns, a silver silo, an ominous tree stump, a farmer with an axe slung over his shoulder, and a frantic hen scurrying away with the words "I'm free!" above her head. The picture is colored with marker and, because of the 40-watt bulb within, glows like a stained-glass cathedral window.

Though I love the romanticism of it, animal husbandry is an unlikely fit for me. I am no homesteader: too lazy, too lonely, and too enamored of road trips. But last fall the air smelled of loam, which is to say, of life, and the September sun seemed to turn my boy's hair the color of a butterscotch candy. The physical world vibrated, and I felt, for once, a part of it.

I'd just begun teaching in a prison where a patch of grass was a luxury to my students and concrete the oppressive norm. One of my students mourned birds and sky with the ache of a dejected lover. They were in there and I was out here and perhaps that's why the light that day struck me as transcendent, and the need to bask in it urgent. I'd have chickens, I decided on a whim. I'd feed the chickens from the waste at our table and the chickens would, in turn, feed me. Eight months later, through the efforts of my neighbor Gwen and her farmer, I received a dozen fertilized eggs and these instructions: keep them warm, turn them gently, and tip them at an angle as though yielding to the earth's axis.

Turn them, I learn, so the developing chick won't adhere to the inner membrane and become stuck to its shell on its hatch day. Also crucial is the temperature, which should hover between 99–101.5 degrees. If the temperature climbs too high for too long, the chick will die. Too low for too long, the chick will also die. If humidity rises, the chick will drown trying to pip through the fluid-filled center. If the humidity drops, the egg becomes dried out, and the hatchling unable to free itself without bleeding to death.

Poultry people candle to determine an egg's viability. Now a poultry person, I hold a flashlight beneath a developing chicken egg and first notice a translucent glow, a silent light-filled swish. Like creation, before it's created. In exactly the twenty-third hour of the second day, the cells inside these eggs divide and build hearts. Mother nature, in her beneficence, then grows the chicks a set of ears so they can hear that they are alive. A mere forty-two hours after the eggs have been placed on their side, tilted to yield to the pull of the earth, their new hearts beat. Life begins on my desktop, both inevitable and impossible.

An egg that never develops is called a *Clear.* One that begins but doesn't continue is a *Quitter.* Quitters are considered ticking time bombs and are often double-bagged and tossed out, so they don't explode and destroy the other eggs. It takes a dark room and a bright light, time and a prescience to decide whether an egg has quit or will continue and even then, it's possible to be wrong.

* * *

I can never remember the exact temperature range for the incubator so I write it across the lid in permanent marker: *Heat 99°F–101.5°F.* These parameters ricochet in my semi-conscious mind when I listen to my students read their work. That 0.5 degree haunts me with its stingy thriving-zone. One man writes about being chased through an alley on a bright winter day. He later tells me he became a runner after entering prison because his cellmate encouraged him, at first bribing him with candy bars, later with praise. He was a hundred pounds overweight and hated running, but he tried it anyway because it was the first time anyone had ever said they believed in him; he ran many loathsome steps, not to get healthy, not to get food, but because he loved what it felt like to have someone rooting for him. Three years later and a hundred pounds lighter, this same man wrote about one of his greatest joys—jogging around the yard in falling snow.

E. B. White says, "There's no limit to how complicated things can get, on account of one thing always leading to another." I don't mean to imply crimes—drugs, theft, and murder—are like accidentally grabbing unsalted corn chips when you meant to grab salted. I don't mean to say it's easy to cause harm; I mean to say causing harm isn't exclusive to others. We all start with the same shocking expulsion from warmth. Many of the men I meet in prison seem as startled as any of us would be to find they'd traveled from first gasp to prison gates. They seem like our uncles, neighbors, fathers, and sons. The reason for this is because they are, of course, our uncles, neighbors, fathers, and sons.

***

Within my jerry-rigged incubator I aim to maintain the middle-est range of temps so the eggs on the outer edges might still be okay. But on one particularly hot day the outside temps soar, and so, by extension, do the incubator temps. The thermometer reads 101.5 degrees Fahrenheit, which means it's likely hotter for the eggs that sit far left, beneath the light. I can't decide whether I should rotate the eggs throughout the incubator or force them to keep the spot they were originally given. To give each a shot at the optimal temperature is to give each a shot at demise. Unsure, I play the world's most scattershot god. I move a few eggs to different places and leave the others, just in case. Then I open another strip of tiny duct-taped air holes to release the work light's heat.

Before we incubated our eggs we gave them names. Leo and a group of his friends stood on the lawn the day the eggs arrived. They wore orange safety patrol vests—these kid-crossing guards who live in homes with well-regulated heat and humidity—and they held their flags and laughed often about who-knows-what. I asked if they might help name the eggs so that when we turned each one three times daily we'd know we'd done so. They christened Kerflumpy, Edamommy, Edgar, and Rooster Sauce. I wrote the names on eggs in black permanent marker as the boys laughed, heady with the power of creating another's identity. They dubbed Nelle, Ginny, Chester, and Prince. In honor of their teacher, Chris Funk, they named one Mrs. Funk. And, because they are twelve-year-old omnivores who cannot resist, they named a large, smooth, white one Delicious.

Delicious and Mrs. Funk's thin light shells make them rewarding to candle. They show their interior life, their dark eyes, and every flutter of their four-chambered heart. The boys love Mrs. Funk; she's the only one named after a real person and the one, someday, who could be held as proof: *See how much we liked you? We put your name on a living thing!* Rooster Sauce is wild and erratic, unpredictable; you can see him move only if you are in the darkest of closets and you turn him to just the right spot. Others, like Prince, are either dead or hiding behind a dense, speckled shell. Nelle appears to be a Quitter. She is a series of lumps that float inside a shell. Kerflumpy looks intermittently whole over time, when the light is turned just so and the looking is slow and patient. When you stand inside a dark closet and shine a light on an egg you see an ancient and affirming beat, a familiar pulse from the center of the earth that percusses all of us to life, that same primal beat Sam sounds while moving his whole body in rhythm to a certain thump-da-da, thump-da-da, with his foot on the floor as he sketches a dragon about to soar off the edge of a cliff. This is how we begin. Whether fowl or man is immaterial; we slip into a Mobius loop of beats and exist. The lit flickering pulse is both question and answer. We are here. (How?) We are here. (What next?)

2.

On the afternoon of day twenty, I'm reading pages of student writing. The collective effect of it, at times, is that of a wrecking ball to my sense of complacency. Debris abounds—pawn shops, lighter fluid, truancy; comfort from the warmth of a tick-infested dog; drugs: taken, stolen, lied for, and sold. There are poems in my stack about war and moonlight and bruises and oceans and babies and fathers and rain. I journey through these journeys, through what Camus describes as "those one or two moments when [our] hearts first opened." One essay in particular is an honest bald-faced reckoning with one man's crime. It is written honestly, in neat script, and handed to me by the man who is paying for a life-altering decision. Early in class, his words were defensive. Today they vibrate with sorrow. He made a horrible mistake at age nineteen, and plenty more before that. He recalls what brought him here, what will keep him here forever. He also recalls the slant of summer sunlight across his childhood bedroom and the carport beneath which he shared his first kiss.

I hear a faint chirp from inside the cooler and I set the writing down. This day, it turns out, will not be a day for reading essays after all. Mrs. Funk's egg rattles. She's sounding the sweetest hello. Her tiny, bright chirp kills me; it's so tentative but hopeful, so all-of-a-sudden-alive. Hatchlings, I've been told, respond well to verbal encouragement. Verbal encouragers, I can verify, respond well to hatchlings. No one is home so I'm free to make a fool of myself. *Hey there chicken? You ready for the world baby chick?* Each time I talk, the egg talks back. A hairline crack forms in Mrs. Funk's shell. Our conversation continues for hours. Eventually, there's a tiny hole through which I can see the smallest beak and a hint of damp, yellow feather. Surrounding eggs, in response to Mrs. Funk's chirping, begin their own muffled *hellos*.

Other eggs in the incubator tremble. Greedy, I count the vibrating eggs: six, seven, eight. I'm literally counting my chickens before they hatch. Most of the eggs I've candled are, sure enough, quivering with life; not Nelle who I risked leaving beside the others just in case, and not Ginny, after all. Many chicks *are* pipping though. Rooster Sauce pips his shell. Prince, Edamommy, and Edgar do likewise.

My sons walk through the door after school and they want to know one thing: Has Mrs. Funk hatched?

Mrs. Funk is trying harder than I'd imagined a chick could. She pecks and chirps, shakes, then rests. Her beak is visible and then it's not. By evening, her chirps sound frantic. It's been nine hours since she first pipped. Her shell appears dry. I know it's anthropomorphizing, and I don't care; Mrs. Funk is in despair. I don't know what to do. I have no idea what to do. I research and learn you endanger a chick by pulling at her shell—something about blood vessels and hemorrhaging. "You'll think you're helping but trust me, you're an idiot," one expert insists. "The best way to help your chicks hatch," says another source, "is to get a rope, a chair and a good friend. Now have your friend tie you to the chair until every chick has hatched . . . on its own."

Still, after midnight not a single chick is out. Mrs. Funk's shell looks drier still, so B. places another warm sponge into the incubator and we go to bed.

At three a.m. I hear a strong and insistent call. I go downstairs and find a wet, matted chick with black feathers swaying upright, born and alone.

The first chick in all the world.

It's Edamommy. Three more follow with wet feathers and frantic cheeps; they stumble over each other inside the incubator. The oldest one staggers across his newest brother's head. Another chick barely holds up her neck to peer at me with her eyeball. A few other eggs have pipped and show promising cracks.

I check the top corner to see how Mrs. Funk is progressing. The beak-sized hole in her white shell is unchanged, the inside membrane is dry and yellowed, and her egg is still.

She's died inside her shell.

Delicious, too, is in danger. She's pipped a hole that looks unpromising. She takes most of the morning to peck away at a sliver of shell. The thin inner membrane grows dry and yellow. Chick siblings, free from their shells, tumble like drunkards over her egg. Am I drowning these un-hatched chicks? Overheating them? Were they not turned enough? Were they turned too much? I want to intervene. To do so I must open the incubator, which will alter the humidity, which will jeopardize other chicks that have yet to pip. But if I don't, the other, the wildest chick, whose flashing heart I've talked to in a small dark closet, struggles to emerge.

Did I not already allow one very alive, very hopeful chick to die?

Because I do not have nor do I want a friend who will tie me to a chair with rope, I open the incubator and grab Delicious. I remove a stubborn piece of shell the size of my pinky nail, and then I place the egg back in. Delicious becomes the log and her chick-siblings the lumberjacks. Not because they are smart or malicious but because they are chickens, they roll unhatched eggs into other unhatched eggs.

After four hours of this drama, Delicious flops out. She lies in a heap not that indecipherable from death, and her yolk sac hangs, bloody, outside her body.

The yellow chick had the misfortune of being born to an inept pseudofarmer who pays, possibly, too little attention to details, who to date has reared her chicks inside a Styrofoam cooler, on top of a desk, with a work light for heat. Were incubator conditions better, and were Delicious not plucked from humidity by a human hand, and were she not jacked around by the other chicks, she may have had time to absorb the nutrients she needed. Or maybe without the help, she wouldn't have hatched at all. Who knows. Now, because her nutrients are outside rather than inside, she's likely to die.

Her life proceeds as so:

Day one: Delicious is bottom-heavy like the Weeble Wobbles I played with as a child. The yolk sac is a balloon dangling outside her body. Because she cannot stand or walk the others trample over her. She tries for mobility but only rolls. In my head, I can't help but think:

Weebles

wo-bble

but they don't

fall down.

Day two: The yolk sac is shrinking. Delicious tries to walk but cannot. She tilts her head up and sideways so her green eyeball stares right into mine. I hold her over water and over food. She cheeps in protest as I shove her toward sustenance.

Day three: I continue to smash Delicious into her food and water. She drinks. Since her yolk sac wasn't fully absorbed—is, in fact, now encrusted on her stomach—I have no idea what her internal nutrient store is. Unless she's propped from beneath with a finger, Delicious falls, rolls, tries to get back up, and falls again. Though she badly wants to, she cannot waddle or stand without help. She falls on her back where she stays until we right her. My friend says of this debacle: *I've fallen and I can't get up. Peep! Peep!* My mother-in-law says: *She won't make it through the week.*

Day four: Delicious stands. She tries to walk. Her fierce effort to move forward sends her racing backward. Other chicks peck at her and she defends herself with vigor. She stands each time, and her determined legs zoom her precisely *opposite* of where she'd like to go.

Day five: Delicious stands again. She moves her legs faster than I expect. What she's doing must surely be called walking. Her legs carry her forward—it is indisputable!—right where she means to go, before they fail her and, again, she falls.

Day six: Delicious makes it to the other side of danger; it seems safe to assume she will live.

Of our twelve eggs, one was a Clear and two were Quitters. Of the nine remaining, only five chicks made it out of their shells. Because all the chicks but Delicious looked identical, they'll have to start over with new names. Right now they live together, cheeping in a cardboard box. Despite doing everything we believe to be right, adoring her even, one more chick dies in the first week. I know she is dead when she folds over in my hand and a soft hum of energy ceases. We bury the dead chick beside Mrs. Funk's partially hatched egg and the many other eggs that never made it.

It surprises me how taxing it's been, logistically and emotionally. It surprises me how many don't survive. A heartbeat is so fickle, and a nice, fine egg can so quickly become a Quitter. A large pile of half-born birds buried in my flowerbed proves it's so: dirt and downy chicks covered by golden phlox and lilies. I'm not one who comes lightly to happiness. I lean, by habit, toward dark. Yet, these chickens! Sometimes

I forget I'm not the first person ever to see life emerge from an egg.

Four new birds exist now on this planet. Four birds whose stubborn red hearts power their every step forward. If it's terrifying to learn that we thrive only within the thinnest of margins—only a half-degree room for error—this a revelation to me too: We strive to stay within these bounds. Despite being left too dry, in the wrong place for far too long, over- or under-handled, living things seek air pockets. Beings with a beating heart embody a drumming hum: we, we, we, it seems to say, *try, try, try;* and even though it often fails, it's hopeful to me—*(wetry, wetry, wetry)*—this improbable beat that pushes and thrums, this beat I didn't know we had until I saw it pulsing in a dark place, this beat that holds us fast on the wobbly orbit of a hurtling earth so we might come back around and back around, weary, seeking right.

The Wildest Show

Angola Prison exists on land as vast as its legacy: eighteen thousand acres framed by the Mississippi to the north, south, and west, Tunica Hills to the east, with Lake Charity between. It's pastoral mixed with razor wire, revenge as religion, violence as festival, and race as fate. The drive there is no less dissonant. Willow trees shade roadkill, vultures line picket fences, and a man who sells homemade knives advertises his wares from his lawn just outside the gates. Guard towers flank fields of cotton, horses patrol in wildflowers, and men spend their lives in cages. This feels pretend. Angola Prison, in Tunica Trace, Louisiana, has slipped into American mythology, hidden in plain sight beneath its own incredulity.

But Angola isn't one of Grimm's fairy tales. It's the largest maximum security prison in the United States—a former plantation—and each spring and fall for the last sixty years, it is a prison at which incarcerated men serve as entertainment for an audience of ten thousand spectators, at a rodeo where bulls charge men for kicks. Children romp in bounce houses set up beside razor wire while their parents take in the show, boxes of crawfish hot in their hands. It's southern tradition. Twenty bucks per ticket. Let's start here.

After I arrive, Angola's PR guy revokes my access, excuses sliding off his tongue in the midst of a mud-thick arena beside fried coke balls and gator-on-a-stick, fifty feet from the spot where incarcerated men will soon run from bulls.

The PR guy says he most certainly did not promise I could tour inside the facility. (He did.) I remember that I made the call to him six months ago from my home in Minnesota, as I looked for kids' shoes before getting them out the door for school, and I tell him so. He never promised to let me *inside,* he says, (yes, he did) but help myself to bottled water from the press office and enjoy my rodeo. I'm not a journalist and I don't pretend to be. Even the public gets tours, but this he now forbids. I'm not public. I'm not getting in. I say *essayist* a couple times in monotone, thinking I can bore him into compliance. When that doesn't work, I explain that I'll write about lack of access if that's what he chooses, but I can't imagine what good that story does anyone.

"Are you threatening me?" he asks, standing over six feet tall to my five-feet-two-inches. "Don't you threaten me." It feels like we're in a docudrama staged in a mud puddle, flanked by the press. We are two white people arguing over whether I can step inside where six thousand men, eighty percent of whom are Black—ninety-five percent of whom will die there—remain caged.

PR Guy suggests that I wander the craft fair where I can buy leather belts. He hands me the *Angola Prison Rodeo Souvenir Program* and says, "Anything you'll want to know is in this book," which I understand to mean,

Anything I want you to know is in this book. He turns his back and walks away.

I follow.

He points toward an old man sitting by the fence and tells me I may talk all I wish with Bones. Bones, a gentleman in his late seventies with perfect posture, is dressed in tux and top hat. Incarcerated at Angola most of his life, Bones is the greeter to the thousands who will pass by this gate. He sits beside the horse drawn hearse that he drives to carry deceased prisoners to Angola's cemetery. The warden calls him "Mr. Death." Long ago, when he was a child, white audiences packed deviled eggs and lemonade to watch terror lynchings of Black men. Bones would've been about ten years old when lynchings ceased and the use of capital punishment for Black men slipped into its place. Today Bones shares photocopied headshots of himself staring straight into the lens—high-cheekbone, deep-set eyes. "It's good work carrying men out of here," he tells me. "*An honor.*"

When I return from Bones back to the PR guy, Angola's sole reentry specialist offers to drive me "real quick" around prison grounds. She does seem to feel a little sorry for me—fresh from the Midwest with nowhere to flash my press pass. She tucks her blond hair behind an ear, grabs her keys, and points to an SUV that will take us through Angola's ecosystem of fields and barracks, the expanse of which is guarded by officers in towers who hold guns filled with rounds.

She knows the fields and bayous of this land like it's her own backyard, as, in fact, it is. She's from the B-line, the staff neighborhood that's nestled inside Angola's grounds. She talks of her daddy and how proud she is of his life's work, how his dedication influenced hers. Her daddy, she tells me, worked at Angola and his daddy before that and back and back or some such *legacy, a man's place on either side of the fence, his inheritance.* She shows me the overflowing cemetery in which most of Angola's incarcerated will be buried, the place to which Bones drives the bodies and the place in which someday he himself will be buried. There's a reason this prison has been called the "Alcatraz of the South"—the average sentence length, currently, is ninety-three years. When I ask if it's accurate that they've filled multiple cemeteries but paroled fewer than four out of six thousand since 2012, Angola's one reentry person says she's not entirely sure *how many* they released in the last few years.

We stop at a brick expanse surrounded by fluorescence and razor wire. "That's Camp J," she says, and points to the building that houses men in six-by-eight-foot cells notorious for solitary sentences that run over a decade and twenty-three-hour lockdown in their cells, in the company of rats.

I ask again how many men they've actually let out alive. "For sure we've paroled more than four after 2012," she says. "I'm pretty sure."

I don't tell her that my people had run-ins. A couple months here, a year there. A felony, a few mug shots, and shame. Lucky for them they were white folks who didn't live in Louisiana.

"Angola is massive," she repeats as we continue on. "Big as *Manhattan*."

But really, it's bigger than that even. Bigger, deeper, older.

"*So massive*," she sighs. And like that, we're back where we started; our tour is done. She parks the car and she points me toward the arena—bursting now with spectators. "Enjoy your rodeo!" she says.

I take my place on the metal risers, among the many thousands who are clutching souvenir booklets. The music starts, the cowboys descend, and since not one official will talk to me, or pick up my call, or return my text, I find a seat in the risers and open their souvenir booklet.

The Wildest Show

This is one of many real entries found inside my complimentary *Angola Prison Rodeo Souvenir Pamphlet*:

> *The "Wildest Show in the South" begins with Bust Out!, an event that defines mass confusion! When all eight chutes are opened, releasing eight large, angry bulls with temporarily attached convict cowboys, anything goes! . . . Riders hurled into the air learn the meaning of "hard landing."*

In the interest of accuracy: The Wildest Show in the South doesn't *really* begin with *Bust Out!* It begins with prayers. The warden says *Jesus* and *blessed* and *bulls* and *amen* and then he says, *Y'all enjoy your rodeo*. Then someone sings "The Star-Spangled Banner." The paramedic lays her right hand over her heart, left hand gripping a stretcher, while

Miss Louisiana steps forward in the press box to the crowd's delight. Then there's the fellow to my right. Late sixties, white, he attends every year, mostly for the food. He's eating something fried, and everything makes him chuckle. Behind me sit a brother and a sister, around the ages of eight and nine. The brother has a round face, untied tennis shoes, and curious eyes. He's talkative. Wants to chat with me, with his sister, with anyone who'll talk back. The sister, whose posture is notably perfect, tells him to scoot down, to find the correct seat. She wears neat braids and fitted jeans and picks at her fingernails, which are covered in chipped purple polish. She scolds her little brother in short bursts. T*ssst*! They are among the few Black faces in the audience. The brother tells me his dad is in the rodeo. He doesn't know which event and he hasn't spoken with him, but he's trying to see him today.

Because I didn't grow up with my dad either, and because I was always trying to see him, I'd guess this brother and sister aren't just watching for their dad; they want to believe he's also looking for them.

Where Are We?: You Are Here

There is a map in the complimentary *Angola Prison Rodeo Souvenir Pamphlet*, but it does not tell the story about where we are.

Angola is formally known as Louisiana State Penitentiary. But it is named that after a country along Africa's southwestern coast. Angolans, for centuries, were traded for goods. In the early 1600s, 6,600 Angolans were among the first enslaved humans shipped to the United States.

Angola was also a sixteenth-century plantation named after the country from which the people forced to work its fields originated. Enslaved men at Angola farmed cotton and corn, among other crops.

And Angola was later a small settlement in Florida founded by formerly enslaved Angolans—nine hundred escapees who lived peacefully until white guys hired mercenaries to capture them and burn their houses. A few made it to Jamaica; the rest were forced back into slavery. Researchers can find little of their belongings, in part because they had to flee quickly and had so little to begin with.

And yes, today Angola is also the largest maximum-security prison in the United States, incarcerating over 6,300 men, existing on the grounds of the former slave plantation. At the time of this writing, incarcerated men at Angola pick cotton and corn in the same fields once worked by enslaved Angolans. And today it hosts the United States' remaining inmate rodeo: *GET YOUR TICKETS TODAY AT angolarodeo.com. DON'T WAIT. WE ALWAYS SELL OUT!*

Chariot Racing

> *Chariot Racing comically employs the principal of centrifugal force that challenges the contestant's sense of balance with a twist!*

For the first event, Louisiana cowboys pull incarcerated men through the mud on sleds. The cowboys wear red shirts and starched jeans and imprisoned men wear oversized black-and-white striped convict shirts and pants. The incarcerated men clutch their sled with one hand and hold a pitcher of neon colored water with the other. They hold tight as the horses corner barrels. The mud flies and their neon pinks and greens splash. It's a race, and two cowboys are leaning and the horses are straining and the men dragged through the mud behind the sleds wearing convict shirts can barely, of course, hold on to their pitcher of colorful water. One man holds the pitcher over his head to keep it from grazing the ground. *Don't spill!* the announcer yells. It spills all over. The crowd erupts in laughter.

The man sitting below me extends a greasy bag of chitlins over his shoulder. "Go on," he says to me. "I wouldn't offer if I didn't mean it."

Convict Poker

> *In this wild card game, a mean, angry 1,500-pound bull puts on his poker face and calls all bluffs! Convict Poker is definitely not for the faint of heart . . . A bull is released and provoked by the clowns, the sole purpose of which is to unseat the poker players. To blink is to lose.*

I ask the chitlin man if he knows what kind of training the participants get before they're released to the bulls. "Oh, they only prisoners," he says. "They don't care if they get hurt." (My students, I am certain, would disagree.) The incarcerated men walk into the arena and take seats around a small table in front of the bull chute. The audience watches while the men play one pretend round of poker. They study their cards as if looking for a royal flush, which doesn't last long because, *Y'all ready?!* the announcer says. We're fixing to meet *Lightmare on Elmstreeeeet*! Lightmare bursts from the chute, to the crowd's delight. He's a cream bull with pink-tinged ears. And he's angry. His job is to bludgeon the men. The men's job is to let it happen. They pretend to study their hand. They pretend the bull didn't just toss their card table into the air, didn't splinter that table. They pretend Lightmare didn't crack the ribs of the young guy sitting beside them. Or ram into that one. Toss another into the sky. Every man has been hit but one. The crowd stands and roars while the last man studies his cards as if he's still playing in a buddy's smoke-filled basement under a dim bulb. The bull circles and circles. Then Lightmare smashes into his torso. His body flies forward before it slams to the ground.

For just one second, instead of the man in black-and-white stripes, picture a suburban soccer mom landing against the ground instead. Picture her mom jeans, her cable-knit cardigan. Or picture your grandfather, in his khaki slacks. Or picture your ten-year-old neighbor, wearing Vans and a polo shirt. Imagine at least one of them with blond hair.

That's not who is here, of course, but all bodies break the same way.

This is *convict poker,* so let's examine the hand many of these rodeo participants have been dealt. Over two-thirds of men incarcerated at Angola report annual incomes before arrest of under $12,000. Seventy-five percent of folks who enter state prison do so without a high school diploma. The average reading level of the men at Angola is sixth grade. (In Louisiana such facts are not public. The Department of Corrections charged me fifty dollars to know this.) More than half of all imprisoned men report mental health problems but roughly one in four receives help for their condition. Black men at Angola make up 73 percent of those serving life without parole. Oh, also: They're parents. One in every twenty-eight children in the United States now has a parent in jail or prison. Some of those children are sitting in this audience of ten thousand spectators right now.

Convict Pinball

> *"Don't move, stand perfectly still," the rodeo announcer tells the contestants, or maybe pins would be the appropriate word. . . . If the bull knocks him out of the ring, he is out of the competition. The last pin, uhm, cowboy, standing is the winner.*

We watch the red-cheeked rodeo clown fake-swagger into the arena. He adjusts his oversized foam cowboy hat and tosses Hula-Hoops to the ground, making a pattern that's wide at the back and narrow at the top until there's a full pyramid that comes to a point in front of the bull's chute. Just like bowling, only the pins will be bodies. The brother and sister are quiet. The rodeo participants in the arena aren't scoping out the stands, of course. They're bowling pins, dodging in and out of shadows, in and out of mud. The bull chute flips open. A bull, white and pink and the sort of frightened one gets when caged and taunted, bolts out, then huffs and snorts. This two-thousand-pound bull charges toward the first man. Some drop into an instant crouch as if fending off a punch. One man, the lead pin, flips into the air. Some men are pummeled. Some run. One curls on the ground in the fetal position, his hands protecting his head.

The brother and sister watch. Three men remain inside their Hula-Hoops, bracing themselves for the bull's jag back. The bull charges again. And again. The crowd claps and hoots. The bull seems angry, agitated, scared.

The remaining men do their job, which is to say, they stand entirely still and take blunt assaults. One after another, they're knocked about. We see the final man—the winner—fly up, then thwack the ground with a thud.

Clowns raise their arms, up and up. They pump the crowd even higher.

The brother is restless. He switches seats, moving one to the right, three to the right. The sister scolds her brother, wordlessly, with her hands. His legs don't reach the ground. He's squirmy. Maybe she wants him to be still.

I wonder if they have any of their dad's belongings at home: a leather jacket, work boots, Sears baby pictures.

Each time a man flies, the crowd cheers and this arena sounds like a cloud of locusts.

Bodies thud when they hit the ground, they don't bounce. This, I'll later learn, is because our bones take the impact of assaults. The force creates energy that increases the weight of the body so when a body lands against the earth, it's actually heavier than the second before it was hit. An assault to your body literally weighs on you.

"Even your bones don't get a second chance to get out," Angola resident Doug Dennis told a reporter. Dennis never returned home; he's buried in Angola's cemetery under a white cross.

Officials once went to Point Lookout I, land of hundreds of unmarked graves, where Doug Dennis lies, and discovered bones upon human bones washed up from a flood. People picked through those bones trying to sort one man from the next. Resist here the urge to make order of an earth filled centuries-deep with the bodies of people who've been caged on this land year after year after year until there are so many bodies the land refuses to take one more. Resist the urge to call it a horror story; it is a real parcel stuffed so full with people that the earth sends their bones back. Resist the urge to call it history, because it is still happening.

And All the Rest

Next and again—reality blurs—bull after agitated bull bursts out of the gates. They are all hot piss and tight circles and confusion and they are not happy to be here. More men fly around. A few wild horses run. Capuchins ride border collies to Michael Jackson music as a white man tells the incarcerated men in the stands to change their ways by looking at the man in the mirror. The audience watches the men as they are told to watch their ways.

I wonder if the brother and sister will chat at the fence with their dad. They're nowhere to be seen. I hope they spotted him. I hope he was one who landed on two feet and not his face. I hope he looked up, against all odds, to find them, and I hope they saw him trying to see.

Over the loudspeaker, a man thanks the dignitaries, the cowboys, Jesus, Chevy. He does not thank the bowling pins, the poker players, the pummeled and sore, the legally vulnerable population that Louisiana just harmed and humiliated. The audience exits en masse, stepping on mud and crawfish carcasses.

Spectators pile into Angola's tractor-pulled trains, which chug through parking lots on their way to far-off cars. We hold chitlins and donuts and wood bowls and paintings. We hold babies and toddlers. We hold hand-carved rockers, leather billfolds, and copper rings; we discard ticket stubs and ripped napkins and empty Coke bottles. We chug, ten thousand of us, in the waning heat to the lull of the faux train. Painted wooden signs on the back of the trains say, *Happy Trails!*

Happy Trails! till next year: beginning, middle, end. The end, unending in this place where men run from bulls. The bulls charge, the men drop, the crowd whoops. The press goes home, and the PR guy gets some sleep. The bulls are sent back to their pens. Men are sent to theirs, too. Bones leaves his post, removes his hat, and changes out of his tuxedo. He'll saddle the horses and drive the hearse—for the next death and the next—until someone else takes the reigns. The sun reflects off the bayou and sets behind the guard tower and the light over the mighty Mississippi sinks.

The Wildest Show begins with mass confusion. It ends with the same. In the middle, a brother and sister, ages eight and nine, looked for their dad among the men dressed in black and white stripes. They shifted in their seats each time the crowd roared.

Human Ecology

When a foal is born on Bastøy Island in Norway, it is the incarcerated men who help deliver it and those same men who name it. Bastøy Boy, the newest foal in the community, arrived last spring in the dark of night, his birth overseen by men whose full-time job it is to brush and feed and care for the horses. When the foal is old enough to wear horseshoes, an incarcerated caretaker named George will pat the foal's thigh and brush rocks and debris from one after another of its hooves. He will do this for nine horses, thirty-six hooves in all. Then George will feed and water the horses before closing their stalls and calling it a day.

Bastøy Boy has the leggy profile of a preteen and stays close to his mother, Ronja II, who is daughter to Ronja, the matriarch in a team of workhorses that are integral to life on this island. The horses plow the fields and haul the trees that residents fell in the forest. These trees become logs that feed wood-burning furnaces. The wood-burning furnaces heat the cottages that are cared for and inhabited by the captive.

So it goes at Bastøy, the world's first human-ecological prison, where I'm allowed to tour and to teach a writing class. Clearly, the men here have made mistakes severe enough to find themselves incarcerated. But Bastøy's physical design—lush, unfenced, escapable—suggests that a man who is invited to work with his feet on the earth and his eyes to the sky, and who functions as an integral part of a community, will learn interdependency better than a man whose movements are choreographed by others, and then only when he's not locked in a cell. When our understanding of community changes, the thinking goes, so do our actions.

Rarely does community accept its necessary part. This open-minded, open-air island is an offering, of sorts. An acknowledgement that harm is shared, and healing is too.

On the most basic level, Bastøy forces men—staff and residents—to show up for each other. It does not restrict their ability to cook, to eat good food, to see family, to take classes, to go for long walks in the forest. Hooch is overlooked. So, too, is weed. The only thing this prison prevents is leaving a community that needs you, with the knowledge that if you escape, you'll be returned to a less bucolic prison to finish your time.

And isn't that a start?

Former warden, minister, and psychotherapist Arne Kvernvik Nilsen implemented and champions Bastøy's human-ecological model. His philosophy is so jam-packed with humanistic ideals and high-minded concepts that it could be an entire undergraduate major, and a challenging one at that. If there's an irony to his approach, it's that a philosophy so heady on paper feels so organic in practice. He speaks often of dirt—as in the dirt of the field he put his hands into when he helped plant crops. He speaks of windows—those he washed himself. He speaks of eye contact, and shared work, and being real and present with others, staff and incarcerated residents alike. I don't have to rely on imagination to know what such presence feels like. He's in the middle of what will be a three-hour interview. Not once will he pick up a phone or check a computer. I feel connected and heard, and that's by design. Such are the very interactions he asks staff to have with the men on this island.

"No. Rehabilitation *isn't* always practical," he says. "Sometimes it is only *habilitation*. But we have to try, don't we?"

When Norwegians speak of trying, they implicate their own system as well as individuals.

And this trying comes about in a most humble way. (*Humble,* from the Latin *humus,* meaning *earth.*) The incarcerated men at Bastøy grow most of their own food and they process their own recycling; they are responsible for not just overseeing but nourishing living things on this five-acre island, including the land, plants, and relationships. By design, the community is small and nearly self-sustaining. Both residents and staff drive electric cars; they're working, always, to reduce CO_2 emissions, mindful of how their actions affect the earth: how the earth's health affects the weather, their crops, their lives. Men live together in cottages, not cells; in every cottage lives a *huset far,* or "house father," who is in charge of loading the wood into the home's furnace. The house father keeps the home fires burning for himself and the other residents, and if he should forget, everyone in the house feels the chill.

It's another man's job to fell those trees, to chop them, to load them onto horse carriages. After I teach a writing class, the residents take me to the lambs they raise and cows that they eat. They show me where they plant and harvest the animals' food. Some of the cows roam the island, preferring a wide clearing deep in the island's forest, beside which residents often jog.

When residents and officers eat burgers together on a hill overlooking the North Sea during Friday afternoon cookouts, it is meat from those same cows that they are eating. The cows' manure, of course, nourishes the fields that grow the hay. (Or, as Officer Halvor puts it, "Let me say it the polite way: The animals' shit goes back to the earth.") Incarcerated folks plant that hay with the help of the horses Ronja and Brun, who they talk to while they work. That hay is grown without pesticides, because it's understood that if you put poison into a body you will potentially cause that body—and then the community of which it is a part—harm.

In *Nature as Measure,* the agronomist Wes Jackson argues that the state of our landscapes reflects our well-being as a society. So, too, does the state of our criminal legal system: The conditions of our prisons say something about how we're faring as a people. Bastøy aims not to punish, but to replenish the men it incarcerates. (An annual evaluation asks: Was your corrections officer "gentle and helpful?") Call it a camp for criminals if you like, shrugs Nilsen: Bastøy's recidivism rate is 16 percent. It's true Norway has better social services all around. Larger safety nets shrink prisons. These facts don't render Norway's prison system irrelevant; they help explain its progress.

Healthy human landscapes require purpose and connection. Bastøy tries to sow both.

"You want me to make someone a bad person?" says the current warden, Tom Eberhardt, not from inside a concrete building wearing a taser, but outside in fall air under warm sun, beside a vast garden overlooking the North Sea. "I can do this. It's no problem." Far more difficult, he asserts, is restoration.

Attention

OUT THE WINDOW I appear not to be going anywhere, only relentlessly leaving—leaving Detroit, leaving my family behind in a blur on a gray February day. My train is westbound for Chicago, but my seat is rear facing, showing *away* with such cinematic tumble that the trip begins with surprising melancholy.

Ten minutes down the track I'm watching abandoned houses with roofs that look like gap-toothed mouths blur into one another. I'm passing boarded doors, boarded windows, spray-painted warnings—*Caution, black mold*—when the train shrieks to an abrupt halt.

Everything is still except the tall grasses outside—they're blowing toward the train as if they're trying to step out of the earth and run away. A passenger groans. I hear music leaking from an old man's headphones like a mouse concert in miniature. An old man hums warmly with his eyes closed and it makes me smile.

A mother and her twentysomething son sit across the aisle and one seat up from me. I have a clear view of the laptop they share. The mother is dressed in a black-and-white jogging suit. She holds her cell phone in one hand, and because she's received a few calls already, I know her ring tone is the theme song from the movie *Ghostbusters*. Her son wears a cowboy belt and boots on legs so long he must slump to make room for himself. Mother and son both wear headphones to hear a movie wherein someone handsome is doing something daring. They are unaware that we have stopped.

It is clean and uncrowded, this train car; anyone who wants one has a seat to themself. Still there are enough passengers that the rising sighs and shuffles create an agitated background noise the longer we sit. People begin to chatter: *What's going on? Why are we stopped? What time is it?* The next stop should be Dearborn, not the middle of the track.

As if in answer, the conductor opens the door and walks to the head of the aisle. When he collected tickets a few minutes ago he was chatty, almost playful. Now he stands here tall and somber, tugging the bill of his hat. Mother and son notice him and remove their headphones. A cell phone slaps shut. The mouse concert ceases. I close my book.

The conductor stands quietly, waiting for everyone's full attention, though he clearly has it. He lowers his head and waits for an awkward amount of time. Finally, he says, "Passengers?" He looks, not at us, but out the window. "There's been an emergency." His voice softens and for a moment he doesn't seem like a conductor or even a stranger, but someone's grown son. "First, you should know: This doesn't involve your safety. In layman's terms, we just had what is called a *pedestrian strike.*" The train car is entirely quiet as he continues. "I do not know if he's dead or alive. We were going seventy-nine miles per hour."

It feels an hour has passed while I've come to understand, but it must have been seconds because the conductor still stands in the aisle. *Pedestrian strike,* he said, and *he,* and *dead or alive.* I picture a young kid about the age of the boy sitting beside his mother. On the tracks? Seventy-nine miles per hour? Shouldn't layman's terms be *train hit man*? Yes, he will be dead.

"Again," the conductor says, "This doesn't involve your safety. We'll need to sit here, however, until the investigation concludes. It will take about three hours."

There is a heavy pause. Then a jumble of voices.

How long a wait? What? You've got to be kidding me. Bullshit man, I'm getting off. Can't we get off? I've got a wedding to get to. Three hours?!

The conductor pauses and looks left, outside toward the grass, as if checking a teleprompter. He speaks to the windows while rubbing one knuckle. His fingers are covered in dark hairs. "There is nowhere for us to let you out, nowhere for you to go from here. I'm sorry. We cannot let you off this train. Authorities will complete an investigation as quickly as possible, then we'll be on our way." As if he has saved this last bit for the grumbling, he lowers the bill of his hat and adds: "A free snack pack is available in the dining car for all passengers. No charge. There's water, too."

Years ago, when Leo was a toddler and had his first real fever, he had no idea what to make of it. I held him in my lap, his body blazing. He mostly stared across the room, but there was a moment of frightened lucidity during which he looked up at me, his eyes full of alarm, and he pleaded: "*Happening*? Mama, what *happening*?"

Some strange sense of decorum keeps us from turning toward each other. We face forward, face our phones, our laptops, and our books. If you watched us on a screen you might describe us as unfazed. I feel an urge to stand up, move to the center of the aisle and say a few words for the dead man, but I don't have the courage to risk looking devout (which I'm not) or melodramatic (which I am).

The young man with his mother stands and stretches. I look at the old man behind me, the one who just a minute ago had been humming. I wonder if we might say something to each other, but his head is laying against the seat, his eyes closed in quiet concentration. I look again to the man-boy whose hair is buzzed around the edges into a crisp cut. He stretches vigorously then looks at his mother and says, "Uh . . . why would anyone want to jump in front of a train?" He shakes his head the way people do when they see something stupid happening. "Three *hours* . . . I'm going to get hungry, man."

"Go to the dining car and get the snack," says his mother. "You can have mine, too."

"Whatever. I bet they suck."

His mother responds with a sharp laugh as if it has been years since she's heard something so funny. I've been this person before, more comfortable with a joke than the raw wound. I might be her right now, and instead of a joke, I distract myself with judgement.

Near the back of the car a guy with thick black glasses makes a call on his cell phone. His voice is so deep it almost echoes inside my chest. His train to Chicago is stalled; hopefully he gets there in time to go out. *Hey,* [weighted pause] *is she going to be there? Every time he takes this damn train it's delayed. Typical Amtrak. Some dude walked in front of the train, yeah, no, no shit. Start without me. Which bar you going to first?*

I look out my window. The tall grass has a long view of the track and everything that has just happened on it. It has not run away after all. It is still there in thick swaths bending toward the train, then craning back, wild and golden and dry; it is not trying to leave the earth. It is singing with foreboding—its tall stems straining backward, then forward again. Like some sort of Greek chorus, the grass gives witness in the wind, but it can't be heard over the voices on our train: *This does not involve your safety. How long a wait? What? You've got to be kidding me. Bullshit man, I'm getting off. Can't we get off? Train hit man, free snacks, suicide, bullshit man, seventy-nine miles per hour, how long? I don't know if he's dead or alive.*

Which bar you going to first?

The mother's cell phone rings again. With one hand she pulls up her socks, which had begun to slouch. She tells the caller about the suicide, though she doesn't use those words. "A man walked in front of our train." There's a glint of excitement in her voice. The person on the other end says something that makes her laugh. She smiles at her phone as she hangs up then asks her son, who has returned to his seat, "How are the snacks?"

"Disgusting," he reports with a mouthful of mixed fruit. Both put their headphones back in and return to the movie.

An official railroad man walks through our space. He's tall, serious, and his jacket says Burlington Northern. His eyes never leave his clipboard. For a minute I suspect he'll give us some news: who the man was, how old. Instead he walks quickly down the aisle. Someone from the back of the train car heckles him: "Amtrak better give us our money back after this." Another passenger asks, quietly, "Do you really think we might get a refund?"

Because my mind has stopped comprehending all but one sentence of my book, I watch mother and son, who are watching their movie. There is a man on the screen who creeps to the edge of a building where it is clear he is in danger. The mother gasps and throws one hand to her mouth while she holds her son's arm; he doesn't take his eyes from the screen.

Behind me, a teenage boy grills someone on his cell phone, a girlfriend I gather. His voice is brittle, and he is rushing through the call. The girlfriend has a new Facebook friend that he was unaware of. *Well who is he? Why didn't you tell me you friended him? You sure? All right, then I guess I'll just have to trust you this time.* He will keep a close eye on her "friend list," from now on. Just giving fair warning.

The fellow with the black glasses whose friend in Chicago has to start without him has come back from the dining car. He stands well over six feet tall and carries a messenger bag strapped diagonally around his torso. When I sat beside him at the station in Detroit, waiting to board, he stared at the ground and seemed shy. But now he's not quiet; he's made alliances with a few other passengers who are also publicly counting the shots they're drinking in the dining car. Before the night is over, he'll announce, barely standing, that he's had fifteen shots. Right now he's ranting about "the Yemen," all of whom *stink*. It is "the Yemen," in fact, who are responsible for the god-awful smell on this very train. I look up from my book but notice neither a Yemeni nor a smell. I wish I could say I wonder what the drunk guy's story is, but I won't think about him until weeks after the accident.

The mother's phone jingles again, and she relays through laughter the reason that her train is delayed. *Can you believe this?* Something has overcome her to the point of shoulder-shaking giggles until the call ends. She returns to her computer screen, which, in my stupidity, I watch her watch. I see her see: A woman dressed in a negligee and pearls standing in a dark bedroom beside a dresser. The handsome man from the movie walks into the bedroom and stands behind her. The mother flinches with concern as she watches the man on screen approach the negligee woman who he touches gently on the shoulder. When the negligee woman turns toward the mysterious man and he does her no harm, the mother relaxes and leans back into her chair, looking quickly at her son, who does not return her glance.

We are thirty minutes into our delay, thirty minutes into the investigation. Thirty minutes past a man's suicide. The Facebook boyfriend has his girlfriend back on the horn; his voice has steadied. He's got one more question: *Just wondering how come you never told me before that you knew his cousin?*

I feel a prayer, a song, sorrow, anger welling inside me. Still, I sit here and watch other people react. I have no idea what to do with grief that does not belong to me. Someone has likely received a phone call from the police. An officer will say, "Stepped in front of a moving train." He may describe the location and add that the train was going seventy-nine miles per hour. He may ask if the man had given any signs that this was about to happen. Most likely someone will say "Yes," with shocked regret. To receive such a call. I've known pain, but never the kind that would make stepping onto the tracks of a barreling train easier than staying behind on a cold, gray earth.

What is our obligation to this dead man whose body parts are being picked up outside as we sit and wait?

What's our obligation to each other?

Detroit, I was told before I moved, resembles a war zone. To me, it looks like a dystopian film, and one the world is largely ignoring: burned-out cars on the side of the road, five-hundred-dollar homes stripped of copper, roofs gaping open on houses people still inhabit, schools sending out requests for toilet paper, businesses behind bars; blackened windows, homeless shelters, cracked glass, concrete, despair; *Beer Liquor Lotto, Checks Cashed Here.*

There's the famous trolley problem in ethics. A trolley is heading down the track. You are the driver. You're going to hit either one person or five, depending on how you divert the trolley. It's your choice. Most people would choose to save five unless, of course, they know the solitary individual. When they know the person, they save just that one. What no one asks in this metaphor, my friend Em once pointed out, is who is behind the machine in the first place? What giant hand dropped us behind the wheel of that trolley to begin with? And who decided where the tracks would run?

Instead of asking whether we'll save one or five, why don't we ask who controls the damn machines? Why isn't one option in that ethics puzzle that the gigantic, all-powerful, hidden hands move the tracks entirely so they're less likely to crush others? She's a public defender whose decisions in the midst of a monstrous systems can feel both forced and inconsequential. Insurmountable. Case in point: poverty of an entire metro area. Mass incarceration.

It's humbling to wonder about our individual efficacy, before the tracks, *and* after.

Again, I try to read. Same passage. I turn the page, but the words will not make sense. The written word has become unintelligible to me save the one spot I was reading before the conductor appeared, as if my eyes are tied to a circular track they cannot get off. I go back to the sentence that I can understand, the only sentence. The book is *Gravity and Grace* by Simone Weil. If I wish to read, my choice is this passage: "Attention, taken to its highest degree, is the same thing as prayer. It presupposes faith and love." It does not comfort me, but it steadies me in the way directions do in a crisis. Because I feel confused and a little guilty on this train, I do as it says. I pay attention. I'm not sage-like, just dumbstruck.

Because I do not understand what is happening.

And I don't just mean the man and his giving up and his body against our train and the tracks; I mean the aftermath. I mean us, in the midst of death.

Somewhere, in the most ancient part of me, the part that came intact the day I was born or lifetimes before, I carried an assumption that I didn't know I had, until it was proven wrong. We cannot be counted on to meet gravity with gravity.

I want to convey this to someone, but I lack the vocabulary.

Instead, I go to the dining car and ask the woman selling snacks if she knows anything about the accident. Corporate lingo for the dead man, I learn, is "Trespasser." This suicide makes three "Trespassers" along this one stretch of line in the last year alone, precisely where the fence is broken down and the track is accessible. Detroit's own Niagara Falls. As I'm learning this, a young woman with pale skin and a ballerina's poise walks into the dining car and asks if her wallet has been turned in, by chance. She is asking, but clearly resigned. It is a gray wallet, she says, and it has every bit of money she needs for her weeklong stay in Chicago. Plus her identification and credit cards. "I left my bag when I went to the bathroom," she says. "It's my own fault."

The concession worker offers sympathy and apologies, but no wallet. She opens a large box filled with snack packs and urges us to take two or three. When I return to my seat, mother and son have switched movies. Their headphones are still in; this show is much funnier than the last. The mother cannot contain her laughter and even her son has a smile.

The drunk kid drinking shots is now at number ten. I overhear him say to his new friend that he talked with someone from Detroit who watched the local news; the man who killed himself with our train was sixty-two years old and had recently lost his job. For a second, I feel relief that it is not the young, heartbroken boy I'd been imagining. But then I picture a wife and grandchildren, and it aches the same.

Maybe the kid's way of coping with this suicide is to get drunk. He did call home after all, to find out details, an homage of sorts. I consider asking him a few questions to see what more he knows until I hear him say to one of his new buddies that "She damn well *better* be waiting," when he gets off the train, and "waiting with her pants down, too."

I find myself staring at him. This, an hour after a railroad worker collects body parts outside our train. There's hypocrisy in my watching, of course, and especially in my judging, but I find anger at the living in my instinctive impulse to honor the dead.

The conductor walks through the door and asks us to look under our seats for a slim, gray wallet that has been lost. We lean over and look below our seats, over the side, up and down the aisle. Most everyone does this except a few who are asleep and mother and son who did not hear the announcement and would think it an odd sight were they to look up and see all of us folded over at once.

Happening? Mama, what happening?

Eventually, the world darkens and the electric glow of mom and son's movie warms their faces. They are slumped toward each other but awake. Every half-hour or so the phone rings; there's *something strange in the neighborhood* and the movie is paused for a quick chat. A passenger snores lightly. Fingertips click on a keyboard; someone received more working hours than they'd bargained for. A teenager whispers to her mother, "I hope we see snow." I try again to read. *Attention, taken to its highest degree, is the same thing as prayer. It presupposes faith and love.*

The young guy is on shot number twelve. Shot number thirteen. Shot number fourteen. Is that even possible? He can barely stand. He was upset about the Yemeni before; now he's pissed. "Damn *Yemen* really smell like shit." *Train hit man, free snacks, bullshit man, seventy-nine miles per hour. I don't know if he's dead or alive. Which bar you going to first?* He and his buddies have found new fodder in the missing wallet. They pretend (or could they mean?) it has paid for all their drinks.

The old man behind me has opened his eyes and removed his headphones. I want badly to speak to him. We are all talking, but what we're saying is static. I cannot possibly say what I feel like saying, which is, "What is happening?" I cannot look at him with fear and sadness, this gray-haired old man I do not know and say, "Something feels wrong." I cannot tell him what it seemed those grasses were saying outside our train, swaying and watching and sighing for hours, while people picked up body parts, while we sat inside wondering if we might get a refund or whether the free crackers are stale or if she might still be there waiting for him with her pants down. I cannot tell him the grass was witness to two layers of tragedy and that as it strained toward our train, it was sighing: "We are broken, we are broken, we are broken."

I say instead, "Where are you traveling to?"

"New Orleans," he replies. "All the way."

"You've got a long trip ahead of you, then." I feel grateful in this moment to soak in the sound of his quiet voice.

"I do, I do," he says. "It's a long haul, but I don't mind." I interpret this to mean, *I'm alive for the ride anyway*. He puts his headphones back in, pulls a blanket over his shoulders, smiles politely, and closes his eyes.

There was a body lying on the track somewhere outside my window today, the body of a man who put himself there intentionally. The driver of this train could not stop. Someone filled out an incident form and possibly checked a box with the word *Trespasser*. We waited for an investigation while eating free trail mix. We traveled on to Chicago where I left the train with my warm life intact and walked through downtown buildings that blinked in the night sky. I blended into a swarm of people, all of whom were dumb to the fact that a man had just ended his life on the grill of a train. Tomorrow someone will be ill from drinking fifteen shots. Someone will have lived through many movies. Someone will have to borrow money. Someone will still be traveling to New Orleans. I will touch many pretty books that somehow make the ugliest pain seem literary, bearable: beautiful. And someone in Detroit will plan a funeral.

I nod to the doorman and walk through the revolving door of a hotel for a conference. Instead of going to a session, I ride the elevator to my room. I want to be alone but I do not want to be lonely, so I look out my window. I am on the twelfth floor, high enough that I can see both the ground and a small strip of sky. The action is on the ground, buzzing with coats and hats and bright cheeks; most everything up this high is still, with one exception. Across the street from my hotel is another building with hundreds of windows reaching into the sky. One room, directly across from me, is lit. Inside I see people sewing at tables—such a strange but welcomed sight at this late hour. Naked mannequins with bald heads and no arms people the room. One faces me with still lips. Clusters of headless forms on metal poles stand in communion filling one corner of the room. For a long while it's a quiet scene, people sitting and working softly with busy hands and bowed heads. Over time, and one by one, they leave. A man stands. As he walks from his table I find myself hoping he will stop to fit a mannequin with something he's just sewn, that he will cover a bare form with a shirt that he has labored over and then carefully close tiny, fragile buttons. He continues, instead, toward the door. When he turns off the light the room goes black.

The Library

WE'VE MOVED TO A small Tudor on a hill, across from a middle school, just west of a seminary, and a mile from a university. My neighbor Gwen, who runs an underground raw milk distribution center out of her garage, shares our driveway. By day Gwen and I discuss tearing down the fence between our yards and sharing our chickens; by night I research tiny, off-the-grid cabins with no humans for miles. I watch neighbors stroll by outside my window and hope they do not come to my door. I hate the pancake breakfast in the park on the last Saturday in August. I do not want to throw a potluck, and please don't invite me to yours. This doesn't mean I don't care about people. I do. I love even the people I dislike. I just prefer them at a distance. I understand that loneliness will shorten my life span. At least I don't smoke.

April

Our chickens hatch, and I don't move off the grid. B., at my request, builds a Little Free Library on our property near the street. It's a red box with cedar shingles, and it has a clear glass door that latches. A white plaque swings below it, explaining that you may take a book and leave a book. And many do—far more than I expected. Even though I love books, and I love sharing books, it hadn't occurred to me that there'd be so many people dropping by to claim those books—people I welcome even if I don't want to talk with them. I am now a citizen of sorts, a neighbor's neighbor, even though I never go outside to chat.

July

I leave my offerings in the library—literary magazines, a historical novel—and neighbors leave textbooks with bright yellow used book stickers across the spines: *Seven Steps to Fearless Speaking. Polish-American MBA at the Warsaw School of Economics.* A romance novel appears: *Love's Secret Sniper.* A postmodernist novel: *The Body Artist.* Someone leaves *Tourists* by Richard B. Wright.

No porn. Not yet.

Books flow in and out as if there's no shortage of ideas in this world or people willing to read about them.

Squirrels rush and bury as if they're extras in a Disney movie. When the bounty is over they'll dig at random and often, they'll be rewarded with a meal. A wildlife rehabilitator I know assures me gray squirrels are not magnanimous, they're just busy. They have no clue what they're burying or for whom and they have no idea where they stashed their own goods. They bury when they have a nut, and they dig when they are hungry. Because of this, nuts are hidden everywhere we walk. That feels like saying hope is hidden everywhere we walk.

Some mornings a petite mother pushing a curly-haired daughter in a stroller stops to look inside our library, perhaps for picture books. There aren't any picture books. I don't leave any, and neither does anyone else. I'm most sentimental about the books I read to the boys when they were small, when my marriage wasn't yet troubled, when my family was what poet Kelly Hansen Maher calls "this one country," a four-person nation nestled in the borders of a 1,100-square-foot house.

The petite mother shrugs and appears to say something consoling to her daughter. Through the open window I hear the little girl respond, "There's not *one*? Mama, there's not *one*?"

August

A different girl donates a homemade book to the library. It's wrinkled and creased and bound by frazzled blue yarn. On the cover, the girl, whom I estimate to be about seven years old, drew a gold-and-black butterfly flitting above wildflowers. Her book explains why our ecosystem needs butterflies to survive. It warns, in crayon, that they're endangered. When I read it, I remember the day my dog died, which was the same day the butterfly chrysalis the boys and I had found broke open and released the largest monarch I'd ever seen. The monarch's wings were damp, and we kept him inside the screened porch for the first day and watched him flutter around. On day two he entered the wide world. The next summer, when the monarchs returned, I allowed myself to think one of them was my dog coming back to say hello.

August, Still

An asshole in a cream Lexus stops his car in the middle of the road—door open, engine running—and takes the entire library's contents into his arms. He cleans out all the books I put in this morning. Later in the week someone leaves a ceramic tile painted with an image of Mary of Magdalene holding an enormous basket of apples. I'm an atheist, so the tile shouldn't move me, but it does. I bring Mary Magdalene into my office, and when I look at her propped among my books, I think not of her but of the person who placed her in the library.

October

There are 1980s cookbooks in the library: *Microwave Cooking for One. Home Style Microwave Cooking. Microwave Chinese Cooking.* The pages smell of stale cigarette smoke. A few are splashed with soy sauce or whiskey or tobacco spit, plus dried rice.

My younger son cringes when he looks out the window and sees the mother and daughter approaching. "Oh no, there's that little girl," he says, this child who hates to see anyone let down.

"There's not *one?*" the girl says, disappointed again.

December

Someone leaves a white knit stocking cap on top of the paperbacks. It's brand-new, with the tags still on. It's so pretty, and

I need a hat, and no one else takes it, so I claim it. I put it on my head and leave a Colum McCann novel, *Let the Great World Spin,* in its place.

In the winter the chickens lay eggs only once in a while, and when I do find one it is always frozen. We buy a heater to keep their water thawed. When I open the coop to feed them each morning, the hens stare at me, cold but uncomplaining.

January

There's a new leather-bound Moleskine notebook in the library. I know it is intended specifically for my library, because someone—a man—has written inside the cover: *If found, please return this book to the Little Free Library at the corner of Luther and Grantham.* Some tips are written on the first page: *Carry: ChapStick (it's good for more than you realize), a flashlight, dental floss.* Those instructions are followed by an account of going to a South Minneapolis tailor to get his pants hemmed. He needs the pants for his job. The tailor is an old woman, and for reasons that aren't clear, she hems them for free. Whoever he is, I feel flattered that this person has left the notebook just for my library—and by *my library,* I mean me.

I find myself grateful for this overture. And, in the way we invest in those who invest in us, I'm rooting for him. Free hem. Happy man.

February

Someone leaves a note on my car that reads:

> Hey you
> You're awesome
> That's all
> Keep it up
> —A Fan

This note happens to pop up the day after I have a professional setback that makes me question my whole life. I have no idea if this note was meant specifically for me, or if someone placed the same note on cars throughout the neighborhood, but I will admit that, as I drive down my street, I look at Ms. Naganichi's car and Yvonne's truck to see if they received notes too. They did not. I'm ashamed to say this makes me smile.

February, Still (Fifth Consecutive Day Below Zero)

The days are dark and relentlessly cold. The last few winters have been a fragile time for me. Whether this is due to genetics, seasonal depression, or a half-year hiatus from walks and sunshine, I'm not sure, but the brittleness feels private and menacing, so I tell no one, not even my husband. Psychoanalyst Carl Jung writes, "Loneliness does not come from having no people about one, but from being unable to communicate the things that seem important to oneself."

Here is what I record in the Moleskine before I put it back in the library: *Yesterday I googled "How to tell if you're having a nervous breakdown," and according to the internet—and my son who saw my search history—I am.*

It's a relief to admit that I'm struggling right now, even if I only admit it to a stranger. What I do not confess to the notebook is that B. and I are weary and barely speaking to each other. I do not confess that we have been this way for years.

I write in the Moleskine: *Carry: a book by Marilynne Robinson or Roald Dahl, a pocket of almonds, a pen. Always carry GPS.*

Writing in the notebook makes me feel less alone in the same way that reading books makes me feel less alone.

The Moleskine disappears.

The Moleskine reappears.

Some wise guy has placed a map of Minneapolis inside it. I think of a poem by Jack Gilbert:

> Can you understand being alone so long
> you would go out in the middle of the night
> and put a bucket into the well
> so you could feel something down there
> tug at the other end of the rope?

February, Remembering July

It's no kind of life, being a chicken in Minnesota. In the winter, if your owners forget to plug in the heater, your water freezes to a block of ice. Roosting happens early in the day, and bedtime occurs when the sun goes down at 4:31 p.m.

The hens don't all get along, but they still fly to the perch at night, shuffling close to stay warm. Herky, a black-and-white Plymouth Rock, is the exception; for some reason the other hens will not allow her to join them, so she perches alone on the stairs, where her isolation puts her at risk of freezing to death. It's unlikely she's just shy or introverted, but how sad would it be if she did this to herself by choice?

February, Remembering May Many Years Ago

Years ago, I chaperoned Leo's sixth-grade class trip to an environmental nature camp in northern Minnesota. Mr. S. took us on a night hike deep into the woods. With a new moon as our only source of light, he spread us throughout the forest, too far apart to touch. He knew the darkness and the solitude would heighten our senses as never before. It did. I smelled the rich pine and heard the soft owl hoots, and the unceasing blackness became my entire world. Something else happened, too. In the dark forest the children extended their arms and realized they weren't within reach of *anyone*. For a few tortured seconds everyone was quiet. Eventually one child broke the silence with a tentative, thin whistle. Someone deeper in the woods whistled back. Wordless talking to bridge the distance. The darkness persisted, but not the silence. The kids reached out as if tapping one another on the shoulder. And on it went, this chain of human echolocation.

We need constant proof that we're not alone. And if we don't see a companion, we strain to hear them in the dark. And when there is no whistle in return? We make one up.

I notice it, especially, with a few of my students who have been locked up for decades. I have to be so careful about what I say in class, what assignments I give. Sometimes a book I share feels like a helpful whistle in the dark. Occasionally it is received in ways I did not intend. Such exchanges are not unique to people who are locked away from the world, though. I think every one of us has a tiny detector buried somewhere deep inside our heart, and when we become dangerously lonesome, it blinks awake and works to pick up a signal in the world.

March

Behind the wise guy's map I tuck a postcard of a man falling from the sky.

The notebook disappears and reappears. Strangers write about their personal lives in surprisingly unguarded ways. My neighbor, an unemployed pastor, writes: *I can feel a change is coming.* We are talking to each other in ways we would never do on the street.

I am attached to this notebook given to me by a stranger about whom I know only this: His pants are freshly hemmed, and he probably has ChapStick in his pocket.

April

The first days of spring bring out the good in me. My son Sam and I go into the basement and dig through our picture-book stash—the one thing I might stab someone for if it was about to be taken from me—and I find a few I can part with. I remember reading them to Leo and Sam for long spells. I take a couple of these old books—just a couple, and not the most special—and I walk outside and put them in the library. Then I change my mind. I cannot leave the books after all, and I go back and pull them out and take them inside, where I stuff them in a box in my basement that I'll open when I'm old and feeling nostalgic.

It wasn't very awesome of me not to share our picture books with that little girl. I can be an asshole, too.

June

The Moleskine disappears from the library and never returns. I miss it, but soon it is just a dull ache—survivable but familiar, maybe even a relief. Now I can stop caring about what it means, who put it there, how embarrassing it is that I want friends, but only inside my library.

August

Someone, not me, has started leaving picture books. They drop off several at a time—some old, some new, all in fine condition. I smile when I see them. My son is relieved. But the girl and her mom have given up on us, and I no longer see them stop by my library.

It has been a long time since the Moleskine disappeared. Just when I've stopped expecting to see it return, I receive a bright and colorful postcard in the mail, an invitation to attend *Wee Go Library,* an artist's upcoming show. A local artist has won a big award, and my Little Free Library was part of his project. I go online to find out more.

The *Wee Go Library* project is a mobile cabinet of twenty-two altered books selected from Little Free Libraries throughout the Twin Cities. The artist uses collage, rebinding, cutting, folding, and tearing to create a "commentary about books, neighborhoods, and the idea of libraries as distribution networks." Because his project is so specific about the address of each library in the way the Moleskine's dedication was specific to my library, it appears this artist is Moleskine guy.

I don't attend *Wee Go Library*'s debut, but I notice that the first photo on the project's website is of a book from my Little Free Library. I see a photo of my stucco house and my red library box and a pin on a map that shows right where you can find us. One book from my library, a cookbook, has a full-page collage inserted of a woman standing at her sink.

She is alone.

She is staring out her window.

There's a gigantic hand coming through her window holding a piece of broccoli that's as large as her head. There's a floating eggplant and an ear of corn and a single word glued to the woman's head. The photo is just small enough that I can't make out the word: Is it kind or mocking or entirely random? Am I the solitary woman some disembodied hand means to nourish with a head of broccoli? I feel both seen and exposed; flattered and embarrassed. It is possible, of course, that the altered book has nothing to do with me, apart from the fact that it was plucked from the wooden box outside my house.

A commentary on books, neighborhoods, and libraries? To me the project seems more like a study of isolation—one in which the subject doesn't know she is being studied. Or worse—maybe there is no study, just a woman who believes she was the focus of one.

September

Autumn ushers in an Ali Smith novel. It also brings good news for hermits. The same year *Wee Go Library* became an art project, a scientific survey found that reading books for up to thirty minutes a day increases your lifespan by almost two years. Scientists credit cognitive processes, but I think it has more to do with meeting other humans on the page. That neutralizes hazards for hermits, at least. It is a small thing to leave a book and it is a small thing to take a book, but it is no small thing to be invited.

The library was, for a season, filled with discovery. Notes and hats and turkey feathers. Crayoned butterflies. One book into the hands of another.

Not all buried seeds bear fruit, of course, but enough do. Just ask the squirrels.

Whistle.
Whistle.

Hello?

Watched

Maybe that tour of Halden didn't start at the restraining table, but I remember it first: blue velvet straps and brass rivets, never used. Intake buckets filled with cell phones and lighters. Poetry on the walls, trees out the windows, sunlight and moonlight and soft light.

He shows me men making things. He shows me visiting rooms with toys and couches where kids play with fathers and—if that goes well—the house where the whole family sleeps overnight in a mid-mod bed by a north-facing window.

"We have no secrets here," the Norwegian warden tells me. "Go anywhere you like." He then gifts me Officer Lasse, who ushers me into the maximum security prison's every nook and shadow.

Lasse—jovial, conspiratorial—introduces me to Halden's residents. Each time he asks permission to, and only after a resident says "yes" will he make a formal introduction in English. Deference is his temperament, but also clearly refined habit. He's a genteel host who can't suppress a grandfatherly indulgence, a show-and-tell everything, everywhere, and a hold-on-there's-more. He brings me to men cutting vegetables, building cabinets, making music, and selling bread. He brings me to the men who take photos, print photos, and sell photos. He points out the men who sing in musicals and the men who dance in musicals and those who train them to dance and sing. Everyone wears street clothes, and no one wears numbers. It is impossible to tell the incarcerated men from the teachers.

I learn (and agree to change) their names: Ivan, Bruno, Daniel, and Jan. I learn: Nils, Martin, and Please-No-Thanks.

Though I never ask, some men tell me their crimes bluntly in conversation, as though they've done this before, as though that's where our conversation was inevitably headed. I hear *hashish* in Polish accents more than once.

Lasse shows me segregation cells that stand empty but for the art on their walls. The most iconic is a twenty-foot mural of an incarcerated man in black-and-white stripes, tossing his ball and chain into the sky. It feels like Banksy was here, and the prison itself invited him to tag.

Ivan, who prints the calendar of Halden's residents, wants to know if "it's true US inmates double bunk." And what's the point, he asks sincerely, of a double life sentence? Bashful at first, he eventually lets me hold the calendar. Starting with January, I page my way through time and faces and seasons photographed in an unchanging landscape: incarcerated men, officers, and staff wearing denim jackets, uniforms, T-shirts, and heavy coats; incarcerated men, officers, and staff staring, smiling, smoking, side by side. This photographer captures men close-up, as if they're stuck together in a very small space. His photos look the way a man's breathing sounds.

Down the hall, Nils and Martin prep for a show inside the prayer room, a space Jesus and Mohammed might fight over for all its serenity, and either would be at home, too, with removable pews and prayer mats. Tiny lights embedded in a wooden wall change color like the aurora borealis, dance randomly, or vanish. They show me video of their annual musical and tell me I must make time to talk to Nathaniel, the star of the show who wears sweatpants and tennis shoes and deep dimples as he sings "Jail House Blues" in English before a crowd of hundreds.

And I will talk to Nathaniel. But let's establish now that I'm something of a failure with technology even under good circumstances, and I left under rough ones. My uncle has just taken his life. B. and I exchange strained texts across the ocean. I packed haphazardly and left unprepared and brought a camera, but no charger. The recorder I packed inexplicably stopped working. And yet I'm here to record something of this prison that hums like it marches on the pages of Richard Scarry's *Busytown*.

I am eager to relinquish all skepticism and accept that there is a system in which someone who has caused harm can get better without that same system causing more harm in turn. Is there a prison that doesn't make humans lose their mind? I think of people I know who endure six-month lockdowns in their cells, and the families who endure it with them.

Can Norway really be that much different? Lasse, a most willing guide, stops at walls that hold poems by Pablo Neruda, W. H. Auden, and Mahmoud Darwish. Poems are etched in slate, and there are also braille versions made from rainbow-colored loops of thread laid out in perfect, tactile stanzas. Lasse offers to snap a photo with his phone, which he's only allowed to carry in the facility because he's waiting for an organ transplant. He takes the pictures and pats me on the back as though we've just agreed to share lottery winnings. I'll receive his photos by email that night with the subject heading "Blind Writing."

My favorite of the poems:

He's Quiet and So Am I
By Mahmoud Darwish

He is quiet and so am I.
He sips tea with lemon, while I drink coffee.
That's the difference between us.
Like me, he wears a wide, striped shirt,
and like him, I read the evening paper.
He doesn't see my secret glance.
I don't see his secret glance.
He's quiet and so am I.
He asks the waiter something.
I ask the waiter something . . .
A black cat walks between us.
I feel the midnight of its fur
and he feels the midnight of its fur . . .
I don't say to him: The sky today
is clear and blue.
He doesn't say to me: The sky today is clear.
He's watched and the one watching
and I'm watched and the one watching.
I move my left foot.

He moves his right foot.
I hum the melody of a song
and he hums the melody of a similar song.
I wonder: Is he the mirror in which I see myself?
And I turn to look in his eyes . . . but I don't see him.
I hurry from the café.
I think: Maybe he's a killer . . .
or maybe a passerby who thinks
I am a killer.
He's afraid . . . and so am I.

***

In the mom-and-pop motel where I'm staying, the front desk is also the counter in the restaurant, and the waitress is the housekeeper, desk clerk, bartender, and receptionist. Tiny candles flicker from every table. A glass bowl near the register overflows with tea lights the same way other bowls might offer peppermints. An abundance of the promise of light. Thousands of miles away in the United States, my mother is undone, preparing for a funeral. And B. is monitoring my text messages, among other things. Which hotel was I staying at again? And what room number? Which account am I using to make purchases? BTW, *who in the fuck do I think I am?* If I wanted to have an affair, I tell him, I could figure out how to do that without flying all the way to Norway. It was not always this way—we were once loving toward each other, playful, kind—and I do not know how I became this woman, in this marriage. I've broken out in hives. Yet everywhere I look in this country, and in its prisons (of all places), lights catch my eye. I have never been more aware of *literal light,* and I don't know if it's because dark days make the light more noticeable or because it's hopeful to imagine Norwegians are farmers of light and shadow. Or that somebody is.

If there is such a farmer, Halden Prison wants to lead that movement. Floor-to-ceiling windows reveal forested paths. Filtered sun seeps through the evergreens and takes the edge off the institution, so you almost forget these rooms are locked inside Norway's highest-security prison. Walls at Halden are embedded with glass squares so even hallways are punctured with soft sunrays. There exists a man in this country whose title is Professor of Light and Energy. This man was hired to help Halden design custom light bulbs that are as natural as possible because "sun-like light has a positive effect on the inmates' state of mind." The professor's custom-made bulbs emit gentle light and only need to be changed once every nine years.

"Keep in mind," Norwegian wardens like to remind you, "he's getting out and he'll be your neighbor." It's a pragmatic argument that even the spiritually inclined whip out as justification for mercy when justification is needed. And if you talk policy instead of people, justification is always needed. Among the students I work with, I know an incarcerated man who ran from beatings and hid in small cupboards, another who lost generations of his family to overdose. Such stories aren't unusual or even unknown. They're just overlooked in white papers. As long as they're here, however, say the Norwegians, as a matter of policy we must fill their time with *something good.*

One writer I work with, D., speaks of light constantly: the flashlight the guard shines into his face at night to make sure he's in his bed, of the church windows that let in yellow and red sun as he hid under the pew. He wrote that after a prompt based on the Cohen lyric, "There's a crack in everything, that's how the light gets in."

When Halden opened in 2010, the international media fixated on flat-screen TVs. Halden's incarcerated residents each got one in their private rooms. *Flat-screen TVs!* headlines hollered. Our fraught Black Friday prize, illogical symbol of luxury. This—more than education or quiet accommodations or conjugal visits—made headlines.

The Swedish have a word for the road-like reflection of the moon on the water: *Mangåta*. For the Japanese, *komorebi* means "the sunlight that filters through the leaves of the trees." TVs have something called contrast ratio, which measures the difference between the brightest white and darkest black. If the contrast ratio is too severe, the picture becomes fuzzy, poorly defined. We have the word *light*; we have plenty of words for light. Luminescence, radiance, glow, gleam. We have dark and a million words for it. Blackness, murk, shadow, pitch. Maybe we need more words in English for *contrast ratio*—the way light and dark are defined by their relationship to each other, more gradient than binary.

I gawk around at the professor's custom light bulbs. Halden's intention to offer light feels like light itself. Light as crowd control. Light as literal and metaphorical policy. Light, certainly, as a practical, more pleasant way to see who you're working with and why. Light as a better alternative to more dark.

***

Nathaniel-of-the-Musical is waiting for me in his living room, beside the floor-to-ceiling windows that bring in trees and sky. He is twenty-six. He's served four years of a sixteen-year sentence and he misses his baby sister. We're sitting on couches beside Lasse and it feels more like hanging out with new acquaintances than an interview in a Norwegian prison, but it doesn't take long before Nathaniel and I worry we've stumbled across a translation issue.

He finally applied for his first leave of absence. If approved, *leave* means he'll *leave*. Meaning, he tells me, he'll exit prison in plain clothes and hit the streets for about three hours. Maybe shop for a new pair of shoes or something? Over time, he'll *leave* for an entire weekend, then check himself back in.

I'm confused by the concept of weekend leave. I understand Nathaniel's words fine—his English is perfect—but I'm stuck on the word *entitlement* and I'm stuck on references to *my leave.*

"You mean go outside of the walls without an ankle bracelet?" I ask.

Nathaniel looks at my ankle, the ankle I keep poking. He nods and smiles at my imaginary ankle bracelet.

He leans forward and asks how much annual leave US prisoners are entitled to. He waits for my answer but sees only confusion on my face. He tries again.

Gradually we understand that I'm having trouble understanding, not because of a language barrier, but because so much of what he's talking about doesn't exist in America. We don't call our "contact officers" anything, for there is no American equivalent of a corrections officer assigned to each incarcerated man, who shares dinners and long runs with him, who knows his mother's name, who works his unit, but also helps him to arrange housing and jobs upon release. There is no "house where inmates have 'overnight weekend visits' from their kids." There exists no "facility-wide musical" that features inmates, staff, and corrections officers all dancing and singing, for there are no such things in American prisons, at least none that I've encountered. And I have no framework to understand when Nathaniel assures me, and Officer Lasse jovially confirms, that residents, regardless of the security level, are entitled to eighteen days per year of unmonitored leave, thirty days if they have children. Imprisoned citizens are encouraged to drop into their lives, to stay connected to their loved ones. I'm tabulating the number of weekends in a year, a month, imagining how many weekends per month this might mean some child's dad came home, grilled fish, rocked his infant, mowed his mother's lawn. Once a month plus a few left over for holidays.

Nathaniel tries again, talking not loudly as if I'm old, or not-of-this-place, just patiently, like he wants us to get this right.

"*Entitled*, correct?" Nathaniel smiles. "Is this how you say it in America?"

Lasse is on Nathaniel's right, engaged but relaxed, and when I ask tough questions about the officers, he jokes with

Nathaniel, points to the side of his head and gives a little shrug, "Say whatever you want; I can't hear out of this ear."

Nathaniel's dimples do not recede because he smiles as he listens, smiles when he talks, and smiles while he's thinking. He's the kind of student I'd want in my classes: smart, attentive, thoughtful, and eager to challenge me.

Case in point, the moment when my recorder started giving me trouble:

> Nathaniel: Is it broken?
> Me: Doubt it. It's new. I thought I knew how to use it but I don't.
> Nathaniel, [eye contact, smile]: I think you had better read your manual, yes?

I hold up my notepad and pencil and he smiles and shrugs in return.

He's a sunflower, tipping under the weight of himself and I can't decide if he's truly got a bright disposition or he's just savvy enough not to complain on record with an officer beside him.

"Keep talking," Nathaniel says to me as he stands. "I just have to make the meal." He walks to the kitchen island in the center of the room to start dinner. Tonight's dinner is easy—fish and potatoes that require very little prep. He chose something simple because he knew he'd be talking to me all afternoon. Once I leave, he'll set a table with dinnerware and silverware and share this meal with seven incarcerated residents and an officer.

Nathaniel takes a five-pound bag of vacuum-sealed potatoes from a stainless steel refrigerator, cuts them open, lays them on a cookie sheet, and slides them into the oven. As house father for his unit of eight men, his job is to keep the place clean and do the cooking. He sits back down and pauses for a long minute. I ask if he plans to perform in more musicals or take classes. I'm trying to find a delicate way to ask how he's going to endure his time. He tells me he just doesn't want sixteen years to be wasted. "I want do something that makes a difference in somebody's life."

Lasse, who up until now has been mostly quiet, fills the silence. "You *are* making a difference, Nathaniel. You starred in the musical that was so good." He pats Nathaniel on the arm in a way that, somehow, does not seem condescending, and he gestures around him, to the kitchen warming with dinner, to the clean floors and tidy living area. "Look how well you do your job." Real or not, I can't imagine such a scene in a US prison.

When the music instructors showed me Halden's taped musical, Nathaniel was singing and dancing beside officers and staff. His eyes never left the audience when he sang, his posture never softened. The kid can dance. He reminded me of Leo, who also loves to perform. Nathaniel's teacher couldn't stop grinning. When I started to leave for the rest of my tour, he pointed at the screen and said, "Hold on. Watch this part." Out of the corner of my eye, I could see the teacher grinning, watching me watch the film.

That student of mine who notices flashlights is in his mid-fifties, but he's been incarcerated off and on (mostly on) since he was fourteen. He's the first one in writing workshops to offer praise when someone writes a piece that sings, and he's careful with his responses to those who fall short. He's shown me, perhaps better than anyone, the difference between being watched and being seen. He once wrote, "Every half-hour of every day of the past eleven years, an employee of the Department of Corrections has shined a light on me to make sure I was perpendicular and present . . . How do human beings walk past one another 192,000 times without ever inquiring about their well-being? They do it in eight-hour shifts."

I ask Nathaniel if there's a conflict at Halden, with staff who are congenial at dinner, friendly on a hike, then one day ask you to get naked for a strip search. Not really, Nathaniel says. "We know they have to do it; it's their job." I watch to see if he's weighing his words in front of Lasse, but he seems more resigned than reserved. "When you're naked they find a way of looking without seeing you, if you know what I mean."

I think I do know what he means. A man I once worked with, a smart and talented writer, was reluctant to participate in our class's final reading. I assumed it was because he was a little curmudgeonly and a lot shy and something of a perfectionist. When I talked with him about it, he told me how tired he was of feeling like an animal on display. I talked about the reading as a celebration of his work (and words!) and the community we'd built together. He said yeah, yeah, he got it, but he didn't care for the way he felt in situations like that—like a prop. In that context, he felt seen not as himself, but a shining example of a system's good works. He recalled that no one ever made any effort to announce visitors to the cell blocks. That meant a group of men and women in suits once walked by and gawked at him on the toilet. Some of the eyes watching him read his story would be those same eyes that toured past his cell while he was "sitting naked on the toilet, mid-shit."

The week I arrive at Halden, everyone's received a long-awaited copy of a documentary film, *Cathedrals of Culture,* which includes footage of the prison. The film shows Halden officers book a man into the facility. They stop at a registration desk, a holding room, and eventually a stark white bathroom. The man strips naked, squats on the ground at the officer's quiet command, and empties his bowels. There's a female officer watching from the corner who is likely someone's contact officer too.

How does this same officer, a week later, sit at table with this man and say, "Pass the ketchup, Alek?"

"They find a way of looking without seeing you," Nathaniel says again.

In the film the female officer's eyes watch, but at a remove. It's an odd test because as she's watching, the camera is also watching her. If integrity is what we do when no one is watching, what is the word for how we act when *everyone* is? Accountable? Aspirational? Or is it through others' eyes that we can play the person we most aspire to be?

I have no idea how that scene would play out without a camera present, but the officer's distant attention is familiar. I'll see variations on this throughout the day. When officers approach incarcerated men here, they shake their hands and address them by name. I see them avert their eyes or soften their tone when the situation demands it. The deference is subtle, but startling: less alpha, more nuanced. I see men with their officers in conversation at the grocery store, the recording studio, the culinary school. *What are you cooking? How did you make that?* They are fully engaged in the way of coworkers, not keepers and the kept. When two people pass each other in the hallways, everyone looks up. That's no accident. Eye contact is mandatory for everyone here—incarcerated men and staff alike. Said differently: Looking is required. Not looking is against the rules.

What a difference it must make: to refuse to let one person disappear before the eyes of another.

It's this finest calibration in attention that will surprise me far more than the commissioned art that lines the walls or the sleek gymnasium, or even Nathaniel with the deepest dimples using sharpened knives in his fully stocked kitchen. Maybe the truest luxury for men captive in Halden prison, the luxury that fine art and architecture and light overshadow, is that incarceration does not render men invisible unless their dignity demands it.

Whether Norway enforces this out of goodness or practicality or both, it inversely correlates to the one indulgence the Norwegians do not allow themselves: discarding. In Norway, the maximum sentence is twenty-one years. There is no life sentence and there is no death penalty. It's never a question of whether a man will go home, but of who he'll be when he walks out the door.

* * *

Nathaniel explains how each unit of eight men forms its own community with its own unique culture. I'm feeling downright greedy to understand this, to make of it something comforting and hopeful. "You guys all get along, then? Are you friends? Family?"

Nathaniel hesitates. "You know, some guys are great to have around, some you feel relieved when they're gone." He pauses. "Like anywhere else."

I want too badly for the Norwegian system to be ideal; I want it to reveal something profound about human nature and the potential to affect systems change. I feel convinced that when people feel connected, they thrive. When they are alone, they are ill. My work in prisons suggests as much. My marriage suggests as much. Without realizing it, I'm treating Nathaniel's experience as monolithic.

"How does each unit's culture differ?" I ask. I'm not sure what I expect him to say: Unit A: popcorn, football, and angst; Unit B: tap dance, sushi, and sharing circles?

Nathaniel waits for me to finish.

"That's difficult," he says. He comes back from his kitchen and sits down in front of me. Then he answers my question with a question. "How is your family culture different from the other families on your street?"

I think of my phone, which I (blessedly) can't bring into prison with me. It's sitting on my bedside table at the hotel. Each text message I receive about my uncle's funeral, B.

receives too. If I read about a woman whose husband monitored her phone and her debit transactions while she was on a work trip, I would think of her as not very sturdy. I would be hoping for that woman to get the hell out. I wonder if I helped us reach this point through my distance, my busyness, through resentments that I nurtured into living things. The hives move to my arms.

"So, what is your neighborhood culture?" Nathaniel fairly asks. The hives on my neck suggest one interpretation. At my house right now, a culture of failing at seeing each other clearly, to try again when trying has become hard, which is to say, a culture of failing at love? Gwen across the street tends to a flowerbed. I've never planted a thing. I don't pluck weeds because I don't plant flowers. Nathaniel's face suggests his question is only partly hypothetical. He is curious about me. He wants to know a bit about my life, too.

Can you imagine if I were honest? *My husband of twenty-two years is monitoring me.* When I charge a burger and a glass of wine on my debit card tonight—I will not tell this to Nathaniel—my spouse will note the purchase online, which means I'm *that* sort of woman, in that kind of marriage. I guess we must be *those people,* though I don't feel like the sort of woman who would live with a man who monitors her every move. And though he's monitoring my every move, he can't be *that man* because he's the dad who played with our kids when they were little, who tossed their toddler bodies into the air and laughed when they puked on his face, wiped it off, then played some more. He stayed up through the night to paint my office in stripes of green and surprise me with it on Christmas morning. He's not the sort of person who surveils his wife and I'm not the sort of wife who will be surveilled. But I guess we are. If it were anyone else's relationship I'd use the term abusive.

I look at Nathaniel.

After a pause, because I've got no answers and he's getting real, he says, "Also, with the *contact officers*? Some enjoy this work, but some are just here for the paycheck. It's easy to tell the difference."

Lasse smiles, nods. Maybe he agrees. Or maybe he truly can't hear out of that ear.

Instead of inviting Nathaniel into my soap opera life, I ask about the criticism that incarceration at Halden is too posh for someone who caused serious harm. That its TVs and sound studio and private, unmonitored cells amount to a paid vacation.

This room grows quiet. The potatoes in the oven are warming into the promise of a meal. Nathaniel stops talking for a little while. He nods. He also watched the documentary *Cathedrals of Culture*. When he watched it, he says, he felt surprised at how everything looked to him. It was surreal to see the sleek beauty on screen as seen through someone else's eyes. He recognized it, objectively, as the place he lived in, the very place we were currently sitting inside, but he also recognized the way it looked—while technically correct—as entirely wrong. Here I am taken by how deeply he is choosing to engage. He is not looking around the room. He is not quipping or posturing. He's not defensive. He is simply here, answering as he's able.

"Imagine," he says after a few minutes, "that you live in a small town, okay? You have the nicest place anyone has ever seen—a big, beautiful house up on a hill. A mansion of a house. You're married to a handsome man, and he happens to be very rich. Actually, he's the richest man in town *and* the best looking." Here Nathaniel sits up straight and offers an exaggerated smile, a toothpaste-commercial grin of the sort the richest, handsomest man would flash. It's such a campy smile that it makes both of us laugh.

"From the outside, that looks really good, right? But now imagine: He *beats you every night.*"

Lasse nods with his chin on his chest. He appears more engaged than alarmed.

Nathaniel quickly clarifies that no one beats him at Halden; he's just searching for a way to explain. "Your house may not feel so beautiful inside. Your husband would not seem handsome."

Lasse listens politely, witness to the conversation, not participant. The rooms down the hall are empty for now; their heavy, metal doors are wide open.

Nathaniel says, "I am captive. I am captive, no matter what."

When he is released, his baby sister will be a grown woman. He will have spent all his twenties and part of his thirties behind a wall. He is serving a sixteen-year sentence in Norway for what is no doubt a violent crime. Nathaniel is a smart kid who has caused harm. He has also been harmed.

The edge of formality has worn off, and with it, Nathaniel's sunniness. "It's just, always there is this gap," he says.

"What do you mean?" I ask.

Lasse is half-listening while other officers chat in the hallway. Nathaniel leans close. He seems to want to be helpful; he seems to want to connect. There's a question in his eyes, not of whether I'll understand his English, I suspect, but of whether I'll know what he means. He moves closer to me, to the center of the room, before answering.

"It never feels inside of me the way it looks to others."

Across the ocean, the writers I work with are asleep in cells illuminated by a hallway's fluorescent light. B., a night owl, is likely awake, the boys asleep down the hall. Nathaniel, who is a big brother, damn good dancer, and maker of fish and potatoes, has over a decade left in this prison. Because he is captive, and especially because he is captive in Norway, he is watched by the world: by journalists, filmmakers, wardens, corrections officers, and security cameras. He is watched while he is eating and singing and while he is talking about eating and singing. He knows this. Instead of railing against my attention, he tried to contextualize it. Like many incarcerated individuals, Nathaniel knows something about the far reaches of what humans are capable of, and by that I don't just mean those held captive, I mean their captors. He spent hours trying to help me adjust my lens so I could see it, too. *Nope,* he'd say in his way, *still a little fuzzy. Thanks for trying. Now try looking at it this way.*

I wonder if he'll be this patient for the duration of his sentence.

As I leave, he fills eight water glasses and lays out eight plates. His housemates—those he likes and those he tolerates—will soon return to their unit, pull up a chair, and lay napkins across their laps.

* * *

Years from now, oceans away from Norway and my past, I'll be sitting in a park with the-first-man-I-date-after-my-marriage-ended. We'll learn—dive bar, gin—that we have disappearing fathers in common. He'll make me laugh. We'll later hold hands at his favorite park while watching someone else's family picnic. The family is large; they take up two park shelters and even then, spill out: elders in their nineties, and teenage girls, and babies, and every age in between. There's a cotton candy machine and a boom box and a dance-off and a keg. There's a grill and smoke and laughter, and a little boy with a bat and ball who keeps coming around to show us how well he hits. I can't remember what songs were playing, just lots of bass and laughter. The-first-man-I-date-after-my-marriage-ended keeps glancing at the party. He has a beautiful smile, but in this moment it's wistful. He says he's always wanted to belong to a family like that. The music, the dance-off, the play. *Doesn't it look nice?*

I'll think of Nathaniel's caution—how it looks versus how it feels. *They look happy, yeah.*

But this won't come until years after I've left Halden Prison and my marriage. Right now, the interior light reflects dusk as I prepare to go: darker, softer, hushed. Lasse escorts me back through the prison. We pass the kitchen. The recording studio. The chapel. The printing press, the grocery store, the paintings and poems. I'm late for my cab and my train to Oslo, but I don't really care. Lasse asks me to make one more stop.

He wants to show me something special behind a locked office door. He turns the key in the knob and invites me inside. On the wall above a desk hangs a large oil painting of himself and the warden wearing blue uniforms, walking side by side, with the sunniest of grins. The painting makes me laugh. It makes me want to hum the theme song from *Laverne and Shirley*. Lasse tells me an incarcerated artist painted it as a parting gift. The painter captured Lasse's sparkle and humor, his nonchalance and smile. He painted concrete buildings, small trees, soft light and wobbly shadows. He rendered Lasse and the warden walking toward the frame, as though they're about to stroll off the canvas. So intimate is his work, if you step inside his painting, you might smell stale cigarette smoke and sun-warmed skin. He painted his jailers with compassion.

This artist was long ago released from prison and is sitting down to dinner or changing the channel or riding a train through the valleys of Norway. His body is free. His painting remains behind the wall, hung above the warden's bookshelf. The top of that bookshelf overflows with mail and catalogs and keys, a family photo, a calendar filled with endless squares, and a pamphlet that says, *Wilkomen a Oslo Fengsel!* And on top of that clutter sits a weighty

SLR camera. The telephoto lens points outward, directly at Lasse and me. I have the faintest urge—imperfect recorder that I am—to tap the button, to have it capture us as we study the way another man sees.

The End of the World as We Know It

THE YEAR IS 1999 and no one knows if computers will cease computing or if planes will fall from the sky. This worries me not at all. Most days I work at a desk in front of a screen but focus, nervously, on my uterus, or more specifically, the centipede inside it. I like when the centipede squirms. I hate when the centipede is still. Thanks to ultrasound, I can picture the bean-shaped silhouette of the baby who I already know is a boy. I'm young—in my twenties—and full of conviction about how I will raise this, my first child, in the new millennium: breastfeeding, not bottle; books, not screens. I want badly to do it right, whatever that means. The small Iowa college town I live in smells of patchouli and promise, and my worries for my son revolve around attachment and his next breath, never civil unrest or a new world order. It is a failure of imagination born from living amid cornfields and privilege in a time of peace that the thing I most worry about is feeling his next kick. To calm my fears, I need only to lean my belly into the corner of my keyboard so this baby can assure me he's alive. *Are you there?* each poke asks. I think some part of my brain will talk to this baby in the back of my mind for the rest of my life. *You okay? You still there?*

January 2000

Before he has language, he demands eye contact. He kicks for attention, then he smiles, then coos, and eventually tells one-word jokes that are funny only because of how hard he's trying. He wiggles his hips in coveralls and baby shoes. He sings along to all the songs and makes up his own. If he is quiet, it is because we're reading a book. When we are in our house we are in stories; we live in sentences and song. When he is old enough to dress himself and turn the doorknob, he grabs a cape and cowboy boots and steps outside.

Oz

He is a be-glittered seven-year-old boy on stage for the first time, wearing striped tights and with blue circles painted on his cheeks. His mohawk is peaked like meringue, and he holds a giant wooden lollipop and dances like nothing in the world ever was or will be heavy.

Middle School

Leo plays one of three Martin Luther King Jrs. He gets to say, "The arc of the moral universe bends toward justice," which I tell him might be the best line he'll ever speak. Later Leo is a heel-kicking scarecrow in *The Whiz*. He's a beast in *Beauty and the Beast*. He sings everywhere he goes: in a wrestling singlet, in his underwear, in high tops and tap shoes.

Pecos Bill

At fifteen he plays a string of tall tale characters from the tundra on a stage set in bright primary colors and lit with warm yellow lights. He falls hard for Slue-Foot Sue and wears a tailored cowboy suit and acts—as directed—larger than life. His character chases girls in slinky dresses, then catches the girls, then two-steps with them and looks them up and down like the cowboys in the movies do. He spins the roulette wheel—spinning, spinning, *winning* in love and money and all the world until his body turns stiff. He's gambled himself to death, which makes the audience laugh. A perfect slapstick death. A small part of me—the gut part—feels ill at the floppiness of my son's corpse as the casino man hoists him over his shoulder to haul away the body.

The Giver

At sixteen, he's cast as Jonah in Lois Lowry's *The Giver.* His character lives in in a world of conformity and absent of all color, until he becomes the Receiver of Memory. The Receiver must absorb the entire history of his people in order to spare those same people pain or sorrow.

The first memory he ever receives is snow. Then a sled ride, a red sled down a hill. A broken arm. A flower blooms. As the play progresses, a sepia-hued screen, which doubles as the Receiver's growing consciousness, projects helicopters and flames. The first time he ducks to the sound of gunfire I think of my dad who heard those helicopters live in the jungle, not on-screen. Leo's job is to act the part of a boy who must swallow his community's jagged history to spare his people pain. His character decides saving one human's life is more important than a pain-free existence. The show's director loans out her actual baby, Josiah, and straps him to Leo's chest in a baby carrier. The first time Leo hops on and off the getaway bike, I worry he'll fall and crush Josiah. He doesn't once hurt the baby who, remarkably, never cries. He does his job, which is to say, he keeps an actual human safe, in real life and in the play, twice a day, every day, for twenty shows.

My son does not fare well in dystopia. When he's home, he is curled in his bed. When he isn't withdrawn, his interactions are clipped, acidic, impatient. Maybe it's the relentless work of a long show that makes him sour, or maybe the fact that he's toting a forty-pound human in a baby carrier, or maybe this imaginary world forces him into a deeper moral consciousness. Maybe this play ushered an end to a certain innocence. Whatever the reason, he's miserable in ways I've barely seen before. He doesn't sing, he sulks. I find myself wishing he were acting slapstick comedy again.

These are the years where I watch him try on other people's skins, as all of us did and do. Leo morphs before my eyes, a different boy entirely.

Bloody Bloody Andrew Jackson

This play happens in the primaries leading up to the 2016 presidential election when the reality TV star's candidacy seems a punch line, not a threat. Before we imagine this could ever happen once, let alone twice. Before it signals the unraveling of our democracy. This is still early, the month the protests at Standing Rock grow mighty, and might just prevent the Keystone Pipeline from going in the ground. The month I get drunk on the couch watching the protests via YouTube and Obama halts the pipeline and I think maybe the people do have power and maybe there are god(s) or good spirits and MLK's arc is real and bending not breaking. My kid/Andrew Jackson tells me his play is complicated because Andrew Jackson was an idiot. On stage my kid/Andrew Jackson stands in the oval office wearing a black leather jacket hollering to the crowds: WHAT DO I DO NOW? WHAT DO THE PEOPLE WANT? Andrew Jackson discovers the presidency is hard as fuck. The Trail of Tears is ended. Genocide doesn't seem to faze him much, but all these decisions? WHAT THE HELL DO I DO? In one scene there's a punk rock solo and a lot of fuming and the cabinet isn't angry because of Indigenous genocide, but because Andrew Jackson can't decide what kind of pizza to order and no one will help him and he realizes he is in over his head. He is so in over his head. *Populism, yea, yea.*

Cabaret

Cabaret opens on the same day that the reality TV star stands at the Capitol with his hand on the Bible. Thirty minutes into the first inauguration of the man who chose a white supremacist for his chief of staff, my son enters stage left and sings, "I met this perfectly marvelous girl . . ." The perfectly marvelous girl sits on his lap, the chair wobbles, perhaps more than it's supposed to, but they right themselves just before the fourth leg leaves the floor. In this play he has his first stage kiss with a boy in fishnet stockings, his first lap dance. He is Cliff, an American visiting Germany in 1931 while the reality TV star looks at the screen in real life and denounces American carnage, pounding his fist and promising AMERICA FIRST, and my son and his friends are in a staged Berlin rooming house with fake drinks and merriment and the actors—all high schoolers from Minnesota—are playing characters who are chatting and flirting and drinking at parties, and while the parties continue, swastika signs start popping up on walls behind them. Darkness is brewing in the Nazi party, but no one pays it much mind.

The hour the reality TV star is sworn in as the forty-fifth president, my kid, "Cliff," befriends a Nazi. His new friendship is benign, even chummy, until the moment the Nazi takes off his overcoat. Cliff sees the swastika band around his thick upper arm. He refuses to run more errands to Paris, refuses to soften into approval for the Nazi Party. In the next scene the orchestra plays dissonant drumbeats. Leo, who is slim and playful, looks vulnerable on the stage with the hulking guys who've banded together in the shadows. They wear leather and holler in German and skulk around the corner to beat the shit out of Cliff/my kid who makes the gut-punched sounds of a man getting kicked till something bleeds.

It is around this time in the inauguration that rain spits into a gray sky on the National Mall in Washington, DC.

***

One of Leo's friends posted on Facebook:

ANYONE ELSE GET EXCITED
THINKING ABOUT THEIR FUTURE?

***

I began with the premise that above all I should flood my sons with love. That everything else would take care of itself. But even love has limits. Even when we love, we get it wrong. That I'm experiencing this most viscerally in the middle of my life is, of course, a sign of breathtaking privilege. He has white skin. He has never been hungry. He has so far only had to play at dystopia and war. I no longer want to write an essay. I only want to say, my son is leaving soon. My other son will follow. I am going to miss my sons.

My children are the two humans I love with laser focus and without hesitation. Everything I never thought to fear for them is simmering in the streets. We are hash marks on a timeline, kin to the same human family who five thousand years ago etched carvings as witness of fear and awe on ancient rock. Prairies and forests burn and grow back and burn and grow back and whole communities morph and evolve and even, we must admit, devolve. Through it all, we raise our voices in song and in lament. We leave our record.

***

When he was a freshman, Leo went through a zombie apocalypse phase. He brainstormed the physics of outwitting the undead, the strength of hiding holes. He squirreled away a stockpile of water jugs, pinto beans, and candles. His stash is still in the basement and now it reminds me of my friend who, since the election, is preoccupied with bug-out bags, those survivalist packs filled with Bic lighters, ropes, flares, dried peaches. They're meant to help us survive flood or drought or alien invasion. He never intended to research them; his subconscious just pulled him there, one midnight click at a time, and maybe wisely so. I compare bug-out bags with Leo's zombie provisions and I check the dates on our passports and I envision rowing him across some lake to Canada, à la Tim O'Brien if necessary, without ever turning back toward home. The United States is chest bumping North Korea. We worry of war. We see too many children of the new millennium take to the streets, march in Virginia with torches raised high, and this time it is not a play. A protestor is killed, others are beaten. Photos of a young black man with a bloody gash in his head are everywhere and so are photos of the white men who beat him, their mouths flanged open in shouts.

Vigilance, we all say. Our world might parallel 1930s Germany; we watch for signs and we see them:

The reality-TV-star-turned-president attacks the media.

He endorses police brutality.

He demonizes people who look and believe and love differently.

The day after his first election, radio stations ask the airwaves what song best suits the mood. We crave order;

we need a story, and we want that story's soundtrack. What music fits our awareness that the arc of the moral universe is capable of *bending backward*? The clear winner according to those who called in to the radio station: R.E.M.'s "It's the End of the World as We Know It (And I Feel Fine)." The rapture, yes, but put to an intense let's-sing-our-demise beat. Should we survive, someone will surely stage a play about how we did so. I hear that R.E.M. drumbeat in theaters fifty years from now—*world serves its own needs, listen to your heart bleed*—perhaps in the same theater in which Leo and his friends resurrected history on the stage. I can picture the militia of white men—*Tell me with the rapture and the reverent in the right, right*—marching in our cities' streets—*You vitriolic, patriotic, slam fight, bright light*—armed with semiautomatics. I hear the counter-protestors, the sound of confederate statues toppling over—*Feeling pretty psyched*—

But before the musical reaches a crescendo, some seventeen-year-old kid will practice the song in his room late at night. Another will recite excerpts of an inaugural speech, another a reporter's take on the Muslim ban and another, the words of a lying press secretary. The chorus will chant the sounds of those who resisted. None of us know what damage will be done before stories are made from the wreckage. And we have no way of knowing an insurrection and reelection will bring a new dystopia, sharper and unchecked. Right now, the country is still unraveling, and Leo is packing his bags.

All that I know right now is that my eldest son is one

second from grown, I realize, proud, but sober—if he is armed with anything, he is armed with art.

* * *

A puzzle: Two young men leave home to greet an angrier-than-expected world. One has a gun, the other can tap dance. One has a pocket full of bullets, the other has just the song for this very occasion.

* * *

The Giver is the play I return to most, not because it was the best performance or a transcendent play, but because it was the first time I saw Leo carry terror and care for a child, neither of which he was allowed to put down, even when he was tired. He crouched in imaginary jungles like those that my dad ruined and that ruined my dad. He learned (or pretended to learn, or learned because he's pretended) how people with power abuse those without. He discovered, in a matte gray world, a streak of the color that we call red: red for apples, red for sled, red for the blood that comes after bullets. Toni Morrison: *Narrative is radical, creating us at the very moment it is being created.* Leo's character chose love over nothing; he bet on the future, even at the risk of death. Thus, Baby Josiah with his eager brown curls and dimples and drool, gazed for hours that added up to days staring straight into my son's eyes. Because he was too young to walk away from it, Josiah was stuck in this narrative. His mom dropped him into the play and that baby carrier limited his field of vision, possibly by design.

Are you having fun with Josiah? I ask often. *Are you going to miss him when you don't see him every day?* Leo never says he misses the baby, not one time. Whether he's intolerant of kids or is simply a distracted teen, I'm not sure. Right now, he's excited about theater. He loves to talk about dropped lines and big dreams. Besides, telling this story has become a job for him, and his character has work to do, beyond affection (indeed because of it), which is why, again and again, he hops on the getaway bike, one hand on the handlebars, the other on a baby's head, until the trip ends and he stops pedaling and crouches in a ditch and holds the baby in his arms. Leo touches Josiah's feet and whispers something the audience can't hear; he might be saying, *A cheeseburger sounds good,* or *I'm tired as shit,* but we're meant to assume he's whispering something like, *We'll be all right. Shhhh.*

Shhhh.

The snow falls and the lights dim and the helicopter thwacks through speakers, and these two kids breathe in and out—pulses synching, music rising. Sometimes when it replays in my memory it feels foreboding. Other times it just feels like a show. In either case, the ending seems right: Find another person. Find a person to care for, and carry him as long as you're meant to, or until the curtains close.

Leaving Delicious

1.

ALL THOSE YEARS AGO, over half the chicks died; their shiver of energy and bright peeps faded while the others—lucky or blessed—emerged dark and dizzy to stumble over each other like drunkards. The first hatch. The chickens that made us want more chickens. Among them was the one the boys named Delicious, the yellow chick who flopped out half alive, her yolk sack dangling bruise-colored and lumpy outside her body. She couldn't stand. Days I held her over food and water so she could eat or drink. When I approached the brooder, the near-dead bird tilted her head severely so her green eyeball locked into mine.

I see you; I see you too: an evolutionary survival technique if ever there were one.

Over time and increasingly vibrant, Delicious began to fly to my lap. Her feathers morphed from yellow fluff to filthy-white with specks of gold and black. She had a red comb and a severe waddle. She was easily the ugliest chicken of the flock, and the most charming, too. When I sat in the chair in the corner of the run, she fluttered skyward, landed on my lap, then tilted her head to lock eyeballs with me. It felt very much like bonding, which of course, is what it was. I hatched that bird. Despite her shaky beginning, she ate and grew and survived. She ran to me when I came outside and flew to my shoulder by way of greeting. She tilted her head and stared into my eyes, insisting that I stare back into hers. Each time she did so, it felt as if she were saying: "Me. You. Me. You. *Meyou*?"

She declined her boundaries of coop and run, and instead wandered the unfenced backyard with Maggie, the two of them puffing and preening their feathers near the back door of my house, until ducking and scattering each time an airplane flew, falcon-like, en route to MSP.

Then one sad day in a turn of events that should not have surprised me at all, one of our pullets crowed. I learned this not because I heard it myself, but because the pastor next door, who slept with his windows open, told me that "we" woke him at four in the morning. Roosters, with their raw, resonant cock-a-doodle-doo are not allowed in my neighborhood. Not even in Saint Paul in the heart of Lake Woebegone. Not even with a seminary in my backyard that's shrouded by jack pines, not even if the house to my south championed backyard chickens, which it did not. The "roo," as they're called on chicken-lady blogs, would have to go. Chicks are notoriously difficult to sex and most people who hatch them from eggs won't learn the bird's sex until it crows or lays an egg. I wondered with dread if Delicious was the rooster. Why? Because Delicious was tallest. Delicious had spiky pin feathers on the back of her neck that startle outward when she puffed out her chest and strutted alpha-like past the other pullets.

And Delicious—in hindsight this was telling—had begun mounting her friends. I waited to learn more before making any moves. This isn't unheard of, particularly in a rooster-less flock. Some people call such birds *alpha hens*, or *lesbihens*. The unluckiest of the lot call them *roosters*.

2.

Our minds are capable of believing the absurd if it calms the heart. Case in point, that fantasy that my dad flew a helicopter around town to keep an eye on me. Instead of absorbing that he'd abandoned us—(still now, I think, *is that the word*?)—I imagined he landed his helicopter on rooftops near my house so he could watch from afar. While walking home from school, sitting on the porch shrouded by lilacs, I suspected he was keeping an eye on me. It wasn't until I was an adult driving to his funeral from Michigan to Texas with my own kids snug behind me in car seats that I realized: (1) It's not normal to have imagined him always watching me, and (2) He was never watching me. And it wasn't until I was an even older adult—halfway through my own life—that I realized why my child-mind thought he did so in a helicopter: (1) He told a story about seeing people in Vietnam from up in the air, and (2) He mentioned flying low enough *to see a small child's face*.

An entire lifetime of imaginary contact was planted in one vacation. At the end, when he pulled up in front of our house, car idling, he seemed genuinely sad when he said, "I'll visit soon, okay, Turkey?"

I never saw him again.

He died so alone that, even after not seeing or speaking to us for two decades, we were the obvious choice to clear out his apartment. In later years I'd grieve his lack of connections, community, support. In later years, I'd learn to foster my own. At the time, I worried specifically about whether we'd find proof that he thought about us, the three daughters he did not raise. When I say "thought about," of course, I mean "loved."

3.

Often when I teach, it strikes me that I am a fatherless woman, teaching a classroom of mostly fatherless men. Over fourteen years of teaching adults, most of what I read is about their boyhoods. I've obscured details to protect their privacy, but the kind of childhood stories I read include details like: A boy learning to rub his grandfather's arthritic joints. A boy whose father disowned him after the hearing. A man whose mother worked in a diner, smelled like bacon, microwaved frozen burritos, and served Cherry Coke for movie night. The essays that move me the most are those where the somebody who steps in—an acquaintance, a teacher, a store clerk—would never have had to, but does so anyway, and though there aren't tons of these, there are more than I would've expected. Whether the essays feature a mother, father, teacher, or neighbor, they seem to be written by two different writers: Those who feel they were loved well and those who know they were not.

In some sentences, love is action. She fed me. She forgave me. She rubbed the small of my back. In others, it assumes an unwavering presence, not a verb exactly, but a heat source, with a pilot light's quiet constancy.

A denial of love, on the other hand, gapes like a chasm. The authors of those essays tread the edges, hollering down—*hello?*—waiting for some faint, familiar greeting to answer back. No sound can be a very loud sound.

4.

It happened early one September, when a hawk dipped and soared through our backyard. The pullets ran to the coop and Delicious waddled ahead to post herself in front of them. With her chest thrust out and her beak open, she crowed. *He* crowed. He sounded wild and bold and loud. Whether he did it to alert the hens or divert the hawk or just to hear himself thrive, Delicious crowed a crow that rang between the jack pines and the maple trees—so *clearly* cockerel-reporting-for-duty that three neighbor kids ran over to watch his display. Delicious discouraged the hawk. In that instant, the model rooster became a homeless bird.

Lacking other options, I ventured to a cluster of farms that hug the Wisconsin border near the Saint Croix River. Nobody in the history of the world, it seems, ever sat around wishing for another rooster. Each farmer who did not want Delicious was quick to offer names of another farmer who might. Farmers politely passed me off to their neighbors until I visited the last farm on my list. I pulled into a small, fence-lined orchard and immediately felt hopeful. Not only did this farm have row upon row of apple trees with fruit-heavy branches and boxelder bugs, it had cornfields and pumpkins and a wooden train. Most heartening, for some reason, was the solitary goat, grazing in a pen. Not a herd of goats, not a pair, just one. Like a pet.

The farmer, mid-eighties, stood in the corner talking to a customer. His cheeks were wrinkled and wind-burnt, and he had a quarter-inch gap between his two front teeth. He held a paring knife in callused fingers as he explained to a customer that apple warts don't hurt the apple's taste—they just make it strange to look upon. He opened it up, and sure enough, inside, it glistened like every other apple.

I stood in line until I had a chance to talk to him about Delicious—playful rooster; nearly-*died*-as-a-chick rooster; runs to me when I approach; eats from my hand; stands on my shoulder; leans in close and will not desist until he makes eye contact; too special to die but too male to stay. I gave the farmer a knowing glance and he did not give me a knowing glance in return.

"I can't keep him in the city," I said, finally.

He shifted his weight. *Then* he had a knowing glance. He sighed. I think he even shook his head. His was my last farm, he my last hope.

The gracious thing would've been to offer him an out, to say, *Don't worry; thanks for your time; it was only a thought.* I'm not gracious.

I stared. I waited for his eyes to return to mine and when they did, I held eye contact, shamelessly.

The farmer's eyes grow soft, then amused, then kind.

"All right," he said with the smallest of smiles. He talked to me without a hint of condescension, then he said, "Bring him tomorrow."

The next day I returned, cradling Delicious. The apple shack buzzed with people and the air smelled sweet. The farmer stood chatting with a customer. Between sentences, he glanced up and grinned at me and made a clucking sound. It wasn't the *bwak, bwak* of children's books, but the real chicken sound, the quiet *brrp, brrp,* I've learned from the birds in my backyard. The farmer nodded at Delicious, who sat calmly in my arms.

"That rooster is used to being held," he said, with what I chose to believe was admiration. Without another word, he led me to an empty grass-bottomed pen between the wooden train and the pygmy goat. I settled Delicious inside, and—despite my best efforts to prevent it—I started to cry. The farmer pretended not to notice as he closed the door. He's raised animals, of course, but never one this special. I reminded him again of the yolk sac that dangled outside this rooster's body and his near-death and his favorite perch, also known as my shoulder. The farmer listened quietly with an impatience likely born from embarrassment. I pressed upon him a plastic baggy half-full of chicken scratch and he assured me he had two twenty-pound bags in the barn. A boy near the wooden train watched the scene, then said to his mother with some alarm, "Mama, why that lady did hold a *chicken*?"

The farm was busy that fall day with people u-picking, people who drive out this way only once a year then head home to bake an apple crisp. People like me. The farmer looked at me—crying in the center of his orchard, in the middle of his business during the heart of a peak Sunday, exposed before curious families and a bleating goat. "He does like to be held," I reiterated for the twentieth time and then, in case he hadn't understood, I said it a little differently: "He'll *want* to be held," and I continued on until finally, mercifully, the farmer cut me off.

I was a mess before a crowd of strangers. Because I did not want to leave this bird behind. Because the farmer was kind to me for no other reason than I asked him to be, and I did not know you could just ask for that. I was a mess because I did not know my father or grandfather, but if I had, I think they would've been warm like this farmer. The farmer, who was not my kin and never will be, smiled a pained smile and said, not unkindly, "All right then. Head on back to your *urban farm*, now, Mama." He paused like he wasn't sure what the hell else to say. "Maybe I'll read about you in the papers someday."

5.

For reasons I'll never understand, I am my father's rooster. But my life is rich with farmers. We find our farmers where our interests are, I guess. Many of mine were writing teachers, people who opened a gate, ushered me in, and inhabited my life, however briefly, without DNA, without obligation.

There was Dr. Mazeika, who in addition to teaching linguistics, made a lifelong side study of Bob Dylan and love. A short man who grew up in Pennsylvania coal country, he was bald except for the white hair that formed a rim around the sides of his head. He wore a tweed blazer, could affect any accent ever spoken, and taught in his poetry unit Dylan's "Tangled Up in Blue." At some point during English 101, he made every student answer the question: *Where does love come from?* I don't have a copy of what my eighteen-year-old self wrote. I vaguely recall wondering if love had to come from love, a chicken-egg problem if ever there were one. I wanted Dr. Mazeika to tell me I got the correct answer. He never did, of course, but he called me up to his desk one afternoon and said, "Did you know you're a writer?" He asked if he could share one of my papers with the class and this surprised me. College was not my family's thing. I didn't know if I would graduate, let alone say anything worth sharing. That three-minute conference buoyed me for years.

Oh, and there were others: Mrs. Nance and Robin and Steve and Robert and David.

Robert, who listed beside his office hours a quote by Kierkegaard: "One who loves cannot calculate." Robert, who paid such razor-sharp attention to the ideas within my sentences that I felt seen.

David, who wrote, "Be-*yoo*-tiful!" in the margins and made me believe he meant it. More importantly, he made me believe he *cared* if I believed him.

The incredible Mrs. Nance, who, way back in junior high, said, "Why don't you try it?" And, "I'll show you how."

Steve, who sat across a cup of coffee, looked me in the eyes, and said, "You're waiting for permission to say something, so I am giving it to you now." Steve, who read just enough of my work to know of my dad's helicopter in the sky. Steve, who signed with a felt tip pen the inside of his book, "Oh, I am so proud of you. And I'll be watching."

I see you; I see you too.

Dr. Mazeika has been dead for over a decade, and I've never seen a word about his study on love. Though I worry that my giving is a form of taking, I send my farmers emails sometimes, small polite cheeps, and always, they send notes back.

Well hello! Mrs. Nance, Robin, Steve, Robert, David.

[I crane my head; I stare; they're forced to look me in the eye.]

Oh, all right, fine. Bring her in. *Brrp. Brrp.*

Me. You. Me. You. *Meyou*?

I searched online for Dr. Mazieka's grown children so I could ask them if anything ever came of his study. His son was the US Olympic men's gymnastics coach in the nineties. His daughters lived down South. I sent one daughter a message over Facebook, but I never received a response. On her Facebook page though, to my delight, she posted a picture of a chicken that had wandered into her yard. She hoped to find a home for the wayward bird, a Rhode Island Red, which she would care for until further arrangements could be made. In the meantime, she named her Henny Penny.

I like to imagine boxes upon boxes somewhere, maybe in Dr. Mazeika's daughter's basement in a split-level house on a winding street surrounded by oak trees. Inside the boxes are stacks of yellowed papers on which young people, who are now old, test theories on what it means to love. How many of those students got it right? Do any love a chicken or a ferret or a dog more than they care to admit? Did any focus on where love is missing, and fail to see where it exists? (I raise my hand.) Who, all these years later, knows how to define love?

If he were alive now, I would want Dr. Mazeika to know that I still think about his question after twenty years, and instead of narrowing in on a definition of love, I've lost sight of one which feels closer to the truth. It can be as simple as a black checkmark in a felt-tip pen, checked once, twice, thrice, over a sentence that came together just right. I'm tempted, always, to correct myself, to say: Wait, that's called *teaching*. It's called *doing your job*. Two people can do the exact same job, hold the exact same pen over the exact same paper. One can do it with love and the other without, and somehow it is possible to feel the difference.

6.

The little boy at the farm gawked at me, and I can't say I blame him. When he asked with his frightened voice why that lady held a *chicken*, I suppose he wanted to know why that lady with the chicken was crying. What did his mother tell him in answer to his question? She probably wouldn't know to explain to her son, *abandoned children don't do well abandoning pets.* She wouldn't know to explain that Chicken Lady's deepest fear is that she will detach from beloved others as beloved others have detached from her.

I couldn't have answered the boy because I don't fully understand the Delicious attachment myself, which is to say, I don't fully understand the many shades of love. The boy could infer that I was sad and that the man was helping me. I held a bird and then I didn't. The pen was empty and then it wasn't. A farmer was kind, but we aren't sure why. Perhaps the mother told her son *it's not polite to stare.* I hope not. I was that boy's exact age when my dad—there one day and gone the next—was an invisible man in the sky. A professor asked me to think about the origin of love. He is dead and I am old. I have two sons who I adore. I never knew my father. I cared for a rooster and then I gave him away. The words "love" and "loss" seem weighty for a chicken that couldn't stay, a stranger who said "bring him in," teachers who said "go ahead," and a father who wasn't a dad. And anyway, one who loves can't calculate. Am I still adding and subtracting?

In this essay, love is a verb.

It bounces off the edges of empty strips and chasms.

Once a student I worked with wrote a story in which his main character becomes paralyzed. The character can't move his legs, his lips, his pinky, even an eyelid, but he understands everything happening around him. After lying alone on the edge of a pond most of his life, a random stranger happens upon him in the tall weeds. He talks to him, tells him tales, nourishes the perfectly hungry mind that exists inside his otherwise dead body. The shock of kindness makes the man ask the stranger over and over: *Why are you being kind?* And he says in his mind, though of course the stranger can't hear a word: *Thank you.* The students in the workshop debated whether the story was too sappy, too far-fetched. This nearly dead dude? This man, out of nowhere, who comes upon him in the weeds and cares for him for no good reason? Do we have a plot problem? Is there a grain of truth in such a story?

There was, to me, a startling truth. It wasn't the unblinking eyelash or the weeds or the inexplicable paralysis, but the astonishment ringing through the character's gratitude. For the first time, I could name a sound I'd known forever—the unmistakable tenor of those who've lacked care and found farmers.

If I could answer Dr. Mazeika's question now, maybe I would say that to define where love comes from is to limit it. Sometimes it appears unexpectedly and other times it is a grace note in a strange place, entwined with feathers or a stranger or another good day on the job. Maybe love is not proprietary or scarce, or dependent on DNA—no small revelation for a devout pessimist. Maybe love hides in plain sight, like a fallen apple on cut grass. Pick it up. Taste it. Turn it over in your cold hands and say thank you for the sweetness. Don't try to define it. If we're quiet, we can feel it; we can feel it when we are feeding our chickens and our children and our students and our minds; if we listen we may hear it in the strangest places, like the rustle of paper, like the scratch of a pen, like the far-off echo of a wild, resonant call.

New School

I TRIED TO BE a high school dropout, which isn't where this story begins, but it's worth noting. I spent my life avoiding classrooms only to realize that's where I belong. At sixteen, I refused to start over, so I saved up babysitting cash, packed a suitcase, bought a one-way ticket in Iowa, and boarded a Greyhound bus bound for Texas. Pre-cell-phone era, my suitcase held a teddy bear, a Bible, and a couple of phone numbers on the back of an envelope. Darkness fell, my reflection emerged in the window, and I saw myself seeing the world. I had nowhere to sleep when my bus arrived, and too little sense to worry. I was running, I now realize, toward a place to be still.

Kindergarten

Amarillo, Texas. I had a solid reputation for bawling a lot, even by five-year-old standards. The year my dad disappeared, my mom, sisters, and I house-hopped around the Panhandle. My teacher decided I was too emotionally disturbed for recess. Emotionally disturbed about what? Well, for starters—*and who doesn't cry*—when asked to leave your own scissors in the communal supply container? I brought these scissors with their baby blue handle and used them to cut circles. And now she wanted me to act as though these scissors weren't family to me? They were gone without warning, and *gone* made me lose my shit.

First Grade or Fifth Grade or Fourth Grade or Third Grade

Two years, max, in any one place, and the people at home changed a few times, too. The metal merry-go-round—spinning under the sun, toe-trail in the dust. The gym with the wooden bleachers, the math teacher with coffee breath, the soft-spoken brunette girl—(Mary? Marty?)—with the rusted bus by her barn. Gold-specked linoleum in one place. Green shag carpet in another. Front porch overlooking a busy street beside a laundromat. Schools I remember barely, and through smell: construction paper and glue, industrial wax on shiny floors, cafeteria meat simmering. New teacher, desk, homeroom. Always a teacher or librarian reading to us from a book. Reading to me, I should say; that's how it felt, that embrace from the universe or the author or the reader, or all three.

Bare skin and Al's belt, the snap, his boom, the bruises. Someone opened the bag of chocolate chips on the top shelf and wouldn't confess. *Who did it? Bunch of liars. Just tell me who the fuck did it and I'll stop.* Not always, but enough to keep us on guard. *What the hell did you do?* Big hugs, always. Al there, Al gone. *Who the fuck did it?* New house, new school, same belt: *Who forgot to flush the toilet? Just tell me and I'll stop!*

Second Grade

Lazbuddie, Texas, population 240. Garbage barrel beside the peach tree, and a bed I shared with my sister. In this school, Mrs. Spencer says, "I cannot read this child's handwriting. I think Jenny makes her *J*'s look like *L*'s to be defiant."

Lenny was not trying to defy Mrs. Spencer. She just thought about other things when she was writing letters on lines and could not make herself care.

Mrs. Spencer made Lenny stay after class to practice her letters until she got it consistently right. Jenny/Lenny did not ever get it consistently right. *Consistency* wasn't her strength and *right* held no interest either.

"I think now maybe she's not smart." Mrs. Spencer decided Lenny needed a special education classroom. Al told her it was true that all those *J*'s were backward, but that Jenny did not belong in a special education classroom. Test her, he said, and you will see.

Mrs. Spencer tested.

The tests said Lenny/Jenny did not belong in a special education classroom.

"She is smart. But she still does not know how to write a proper *J*."

Seventh Grade

Plains, Texas. The duplex on the outskirts of town under the shadow of the water tower. The year I met tarantulas. This one stands out in memory, because the people were so good, because it was there I met Mrs. Nance, and there she introduced me to myself. Scorpions on the walls, grasshoppers lining the streets. Our Volkswagen Rabbit in the land of SUVs, our stretched vowels. We weren't Baptist or born again, or even wearing boots. Hours you'd find me wandering the field—dried grass for miles, vast sky above—picking up horned toads, climbing the water tower, B-team sports, last-seat band, reading, retreating. This little town revolved around athletics, and I preferred the art of doing nothing to playing sports badly. Mrs. Nance—small, sweetly stern, starched shirts, straight skirts—had other ideas. *Please enter the UIL writing contest,* she said. I did. And then I won first place. I *won* something? Bawling Lenny/Jenny won on behalf of the school, and people noticed with an approving tone? *Hey, nice work, kid,* Mrs. Nance said, the volleyball players said, Al said, even Coach P. (who benched me) said.

High School(s)

Hello, Lubbock. Hello, Wilson Junior High, Coronado High. Hello, first love. Hello, best park in the world, where my crush played basketball. Goodbye, Lubbock. Goodbye, locker. Goodbye, Wilson Junior High, Coronado High; goodbye, first love who made me laugh; goodbye, new/old bedroom with the sliding plywood door; goodbye, dear friend with the prettiest soprano, who gifted me that teddy bear whose T-shirt said: *Somebody in Texas Loves You.*

Hey again, U-Haul, into which I packed a love letter, that teddy bear, and self-pity.

Junior Year

A police car intercepted the Greyhound sometime after midnight, somewhere in Missouri, alongside Mom and Al, who hauled me back to our apartment, third floor end of the hall. Meanwhile, each time the bell rang on a hill in Iowa a mile from the bus stop, teachers called my name, but no one responded. I physically could not start over. I took a month off until I saw no way but to finish.

In the early days I thought I'd rather be hit by a car on the way to school than spend one more day trying to know new people or helping them to know me. I craved the feeling of a house that never changed, in a place where people stayed.

Often, with scrounged lunch-money quarters in my pocket, I circled the city in the family's Chevy until I could sneak back to our apartment and fake-cough. I was absent as much as I was present, and because of that, my final years of the new-to-me Catholic school were rough. I received exactly zero points in geometry after answering exactly zero questions on each assignment. My entire life at that time mirrored geometry class, with one exception: English.

I took the school's Great Books Course, which my GPA did not qualify me for, but only after petitioning the teacher, repeatedly. Sister Dream Crusher stuffed her hankie up her blousy sleeve, told me my makeup was ugly (*wipe off your face*), and said she enrolled students on an invite-only basis—college level, for advanced students—and based on my "credentials," that was not me. Normally when the world said *not for you,* I believed it. But I carried Mrs. Nance's insistence, and a little town's congratulations from years past. Channeling Al's advocacy, I pointed to standardized test scores as a last-ditch qualification and Dream Crusher relented. She awarded only one A per class, per gender, and that year the "girls'" A went to me. Most importantly, I immersed myself in challenging books and conversations about them, which is to say, I found a reason to go to school.

College

I wanted a life in language. To make that happen, I would need college. And money. Sitting on orange shag carpet filling out financial aid questions that were overwhelming and detailed and demanding information I didn't know and didn't know how to find, I took what I was sure was a sign from the universe. I crumpled up the application. No one in my family had earned a college degree. Why would I be the first to start? I turned to B., the man who became my husband, and I told him college is the sort of thing other kinds of people do, not the sort of thing *I* do.

B.—who was acing college, whose parents and siblings had, too—took the application from the wastebasket and smoothed it out. He insisted college didn't require divine intervention, just follow-through. As in, *follow through on the financial aid application.*

Nights I sat in the radiator-heated classrooms that held my classmates' fresh poems. Days I read novels and memoirs and poems. I earned a 4.0 my first semester. Oh, and I married him. Too young and too fast. It was still one of the happiest years of my life. We put a bed in our kitchen and my books on the windowsill. We made a home in our studio apartment, and I left that apartment to walk across campus to so many writing workshops that my college advisor admonished me at registration time: You have to take other classes, you realize? *To graduate?*

Introduction to Creative Writing: Lino Lakes Prison

Decades later, I've graduated three times over, and leading workshop after workshop is part of my job. I asked my initial class of writing students to tell me about the first thing they could remember writing or reading that meant a lot to them. Many remembered poems they'd written as kids. One, in particular, was a poem a forty-year-old man, D., wrote to his dad at age ten. He still recited it from memory: "You don't have to be perfect, you just have to show up." J., locked up for twenty years already, talked about his childhood baseball stored in his mother's attic, and a poem he'd written with the refrain *please don't throw it away.* D. shared how the smell of new carpet made him homesick for a place that he left long ago, that no longer exists. He wondered, through his writing, whether he would share that reflection with the class or pretend to be someone who didn't care. Yet another man explained that reading Robinson Crusoe made him realize how fortunate he was to have what little he did have: food, a roof, an occasional blue sky. This was in the first twenty minutes of the first class.

I knew in that moment I did not want to teach anywhere else and, for the most part, I have not.

Fifth Grade and Third, Take Two

I wanted to give them a nest, to the extent that I knew how, so we stayed in the same house in the same neighborhood in the same town. The year I started teaching and for years after, the kids and I walked each morning to school: down the curved street, past the seminary, over to Como, past the Speedy Mart, through sun or subzero temps. Hello, Rhona and Jonathan and Anthony, who also walk this path. Hello, crossing guards, holding the same orange flags: *attention, alert, cross,* singsong in unison. Hello, same cafeteria, little school hallways, shined and smelling of glue.

Introduction to Creative Writing: Lino Lakes Prison, Stillwater Prison, Moose Lake Prison, Shakopee Prison, Faribault Prison

Writers and their notebooks. Mentees and their packets. Pencil-tapping and jokes. Kelly and Nico and Dain and Peter and Wendy and Nell joined me walking into classrooms, and eighty or so writers joined us, among them EZ, b, Bino, David, Paulo, Don, K., P., J., Von, CF, Foom, Amenya. Under fluorescent lights and cameras, we read Espada and practiced anaphora with his *Alabanza*. We read Baldwin. We wrote about what our parents carried (guilt, guns, cigarettes, sorrow). We sat in circles and shared what was tender and real. We read Tranströmer: “Every person is a half-open door / leading to a room for everyone.”

PhD in Gone

Enroll twelve students, and absence will fill another four to six slots. *Missing* manspreads beside us. *Gone* slips into white space and the simplest memories: birthday bacon, slamming door, no call, frybread, no visit, dirt road, whiskey-breath, slamming door.

Incarcerated writers are this country's foremost absence experts. They populate lost generations inside composition notebooks, fathers especially. *Missing fathers* is not a cliché as some editor on a panel once declared, it is an *epidemic*. So much so that absent fathers need their own collective noun: A *murder* of crows. A *brood* of chickens. A *haunt* of fathers. In the face of that epidemic, writers I work with find ingenious craft solutions to outline absence: artifacts, oral histories, speculative imagining, and negative space. Their collective conjuring, a haunted genre. Is it possible to bear witness to their missing in the margins? *What did you imagine he wore? What might he have said if he'd been there?*

School of My Subconscious

My recurring nightmare for decades embarrasses me with its simplicity. I travel a great distance from Somewhere to Texas to visit my dad for the first time in over twenty years, but he does not answer the door. I stand on the porch of a white brick duplex while my car idles on the street. I ring the doorbell, then look down at my feet on the concrete step. I'm wearing striped canvas shoes with thin soles and I tap my feet.

I ring. I wait.

The doorbell chimes inside the house, but no one comes to the door.

I ring. I wait.

The doorbell chimes. No movement.

It is clear he is home.

I feel him watching me, but I pretend otherwise.

Again, I ring and again, I wait. My feet stand on cold steps.

After a long pause, I look to the window, and I see a blue eye peek through the bent metal blinds in the bottom right corner. He's clearly there. He sees me.

The blinds slide down, but the door does not open.

That's when I understand in every part of my body that he will never answer.

The feeling I had in the dream was resignation. A little shrug: *That's okay. I know you can't answer! No worries! I'll just go back to my car.*

I'm no shrink, but that seems like the scariest response of all. It doesn't bode well for that dream-kid in a future real world.

Seven years into teaching, seven years into writing notes in the margins to students who made generations of absent dads materialize on the page, my dream stopped. My recurring dream vanished, and a productive anger slipped into its place. You might even call it a vindictive love, of the sort that says: *It's not that fucking hard. We'll show up for each other. Here: Look at how it's done.*

Advanced Creative Writing: Lino Lakes Prison, Stillwater Prison, Moose Lake Prison, Shakopee Prison, Faribault Prison, Rush City Prison, Oak Park Heights Prison

How're you doing? Alive and breathing! Knee-tapping beneath the table, dust motes in the air, we circle up and settle again and again into words. Words hush the feet shuffling in the hallway outside our door, hush fights with family, hush the walkie-talkie on our table, hush the fear, hush our nervous systems' isolation. It's tense, some of this sharing, but we do it, and we see each other and the world better and in our understanding we feel closer and in our closeness we reach for humor, so we laugh a lot, so we get dopamine and serotonin and endorphins so this classroom space—this community—feels good *so we are careful with each other* so we can come back so we can share more stories and feel connected to others and the larger world.

At the end of the night, we pass out our feedback, thank-you notes, revisions. We shake hands, and they say, *Drive safely! Thanks for coming in. Can you see if they'll let us have cheesecake at the reading?*

I drive off and—even after fourteen years of teaching—I still want to tell the whole world how much talent I get to see, how bright and startling and weird and wanting we all are. These writers, especially, are so generous to each other: pointing out each other's talent, open, willing to be moved, ready to find awe. Their kindness is automatic, even enthusiastic. Though I'm a cynic by nature, it's a gift to feel connected to something undeniably real and good.

This caring happens to take place in classrooms, but it doesn't really matter where or why. What matters is that it happens reliably, year after year, and here's the real kicker: It is a joy, not an obligation. Generational trauma, unwound, at least for some of us. That's a hell of a pattern to break. A small human miracle brought to you by a poem, handwritten on composition paper.

School of Hypocrisy and Change

Don't give up! I say to writers I have worked with for over a decade. Many don't, publishing poems and essays and whole damn books. How I say so with a straight face while doubting myself, I don't know. *Blah blah bravery.* Charlie Brown's teacher, *waah waah.* I give advice I don't follow. *Write what you wish to avoid.* I even offer techniques. If that's too hard? *Start in third person.* I am not as brave as them, not by a long shot. I should follow my own prompts once in a while.

~~I get stuck. I I I~~
She wrote for years at five a.m. in the pitch black, with the great horned owl, and the snow, and the radiator, and the wind thwacking the red scrap stuck high in the pine tree outside her window while her sons slept. Her sentences roamed the alleys of her back brain. Her paragraphs resurrected empty beer cans and dads who hurt kids. Her stories found even love to have jagged edges. Her husband, the one who straightened out that crumpled application with his own hands, who meant it at the time, he really did, tossed one of

her stories onto the table. In the story, a husband monitored a wife.

"Do you have a problem with men?"

He stopped attending her readings, but monitored her every word. After she went to bed each night, he opened her laptop and read emails, texts, the sentences in this book. Sometimes she changed the font color to white so she could write without seeing every word through his lens. When he opened a document, it looked blank as can be. Beneath the white space,

she wrote uncensored.

Not so long ago they were twenty-two, kids in the wild world, constructing a new definition of home. She loved the way he sang when he played guitar, pausing each time he switched cords, high and soft, even unsteady—he always finished the song. The bouquet of daisies he bought to celebrate her college graduation, the photo of that bouquet snug in a small black frame, a reminder of all the times he had her back. Every time she looked at that photo, she remembered him smoothing out that application, handing over a pen. But when she used that pen with confidence, he expected it back.

One time too many, in scenes she won't recount, using words that could never be unspoken, it became clear their contract had changed. It seemed to her (though he would disagree) that he would support her smallness, but not her striving. She no longer wanted to accept *This is not for you.* She would not go back to *What the hell did you do?* And she did not owe an answer to the question *Who the fuck do you think you are?*

School of Life

I hear the copy machine humming down the hall. It's the end of the week, on a crisp fall day, thirteen years after the first class. I remember J.'s voice and that copy machine—*over here, over here, kachunk, kachunk*—and I picture his baseball still waiting in his mom's attic. Mrs. Nance, from the treeless Texas Panhandle, didn't come to mind when I taught that first class—how funny, because now I can't unsee her teacher DNA woven deep throughout my entire life, that threaded gold strand offering goodness, a shock of beauty, saying, *Sturdiness is for you, too.*

We're a strange school, a tiny community on a map in this chilly metro, this northern state, but we've built a space inside which we can live large, larger than our disappointments and larger than the smallest version of ourselves, this in the face of people who couldn't be present for the many versions of us in a country that engineers disappearing. A portal through which to offer love and to receive it. To demand to be seen, not just surveilled. That's the most freeing thing I can imagine, coming out of the most confined space on earth.

This book, the one you're holding in your hands, has taken years to write. Partly because raising kids takes time. Building community takes time. Because divorce will waylay progress and decimate your life and the lives of those you love. Because while I was writing it, I learned that books matter, but not as much as the places writing them takes you and the people it brings you.

Every person is a half-open door / leading to a room for everyone. Absence, in this way, exponentially erased. Our rooms, as a result—endless? I like to think my room for everyone is some combination of all the houses I have lived in but lost, moved out of, and loved. A bay window overlooking a dry grass field. A basketball court with blue rims. The first house we owned together, the wood floor he discovered under the brown shag, then painted baby blue. A stucco Tudor on a curved street with wooden stairs, worn from the feet of two growing boys. And the classrooms I work in now—they are home to me, too.

Why does it take so long to learn to build something without demolishing yourself? I did not know how to do that when I was sixteen, or even, I'm so sorry, when I was twenty-two. But now I do. A life's work: building a room that keeps us whole, and still lets others in. Now when someone approaches, it is vast enough, and peopled enough, and raucous and safe enough, that when they knock, someone always opens a goddamn door. I grieve for those who are gone or not knocking. I probably always will. Every human who shaped us exists inside this space: in the open door and the breeze, in our sentences and our stanzas, in our white space and in our turns. In each beginning, and even our ends.

Night Cows

For E. and S.

With thanks to Todd Hido and Maggie Steber

THE COWS SHOWED UP just as the world began to end. They were there when I returned to Minnesota from Manhattan, where I'd gone to pick up Leo after his spring semester had been canceled. As a single parent with full custody of two kids, I had little time to spare. The day I left, I slid a pork shoulder into the oven for the Sam, then loaded up on crackers and coffee so I could drive solo to retrieve the older boy. Because I was passing through Philadelphia, I also picked up his ex-girlfriend, my bonus child, who, a few days later, spiked a fever, then began exhibiting symptoms of Covid.

There are forty or so cows, seven calves, and no bulls. They're dairy cows, the type of black-and-white beauties you might see lounging on the green hillsides of Wisconsin or dotting the winding backroads of Upstate New York. They wear white plastic ear tags stamped with four-digit numbers. Their barn, which is located a mile from my house in the far corner of a university campus, has beds of hay in the back and a concrete trough at the front, but it looks less like a barn than a carport filled with cows. Their pens are open, so the cows get up and follow my dog Toby and me along the fence if there is no food in their trough and the day is long. Toby somehow understands to be gentle with them when they amble over. The cows first seemed to view me as secondary—just the thing holding onto the dog—but they have since learned that I can pet them and the dog cannot. The cows and Toby do lick each other's tongues. I call this kissing, though to the animals it is probably something different. The cows' tongues are spiraling and salt-seeking, secret muscles that move like dancers.

The prisons are locked down, so I can't go inside to work with my students, most of whom I've known for over a decade. Not only do the writers no longer have classes, they cannot have visitors either: no moms, no daughters, no brothers, no beloveds. Through word of mouth I hear how they are faring. Thankfully, my students are all still well, but the virus has brought a disruption to their routine, and for some, it has brought terror. One man, whom I consider a friend, wants his story to be part of the public record. He wants to tell the world what the pandemic is like for him, a caged man who lived through the Cambodian genocide. When the Khmer Rouge came, he says, "I was thirteen and at school. My family fled their home but couldn't find me. I was lost. But even in this moment, my dad risked his life to return home to unlatch the gate that kept our hogs penned in. He knew the pigs would die if they were locked in the cage and he wasn't there to feed them, to care for them. I wonder: With Covid coming into the prisons like the Khmer Rouge, will we be forgotten in our pens? Who will remember the prisoners in a time like this?"

I can send him a note about a class, but I am not allowed to send him a personal note. If I could, I would say, *We will memorialize you if you die. We will tell your loved ones we also loved you, and we will tell them why. We are thinking of you daily.*

Leo's ex is now quarantined in my basement with what we think is a mild case of Covid. Because it is early in the pandemic, when tests are only for sports teams and the dying, we cannot be certain. The uncertainty leaves room for doubt. Most of the time I am numb, and when I slide out of denial, I tell myself that we nearly bathed in hand sanitizer while smooshed together on the car ride. I tell myself that she's too young to develop serious symptoms. She is often upright and, to my relief, sassy enough to ask me to stop checking on her so often. I allow myself to believe that if this is how the virus hits the young, she and my kids will be all right. As for me, I make contingency plans in my head: How far could the boys stretch my pittance of life insurance? Would the one who knows how to cook feed the one who refuses to learn? But we are not at that point and likely won't get there.

A week ago, as I drove to Manhattan, she pinged my phone hourly to make sure I hadn't changed my mind about giving her a ride. It was eerie in her suddenly empty dorm, she said. Now, I overhear her tell an instructor on a screen that she is too sick to sing—and, by the way, also quarantined with her ex and his mom.

The calves suck my coat sleeve and attempt to eat the cardigan tied around my waist. A few cows sniff my hand when I extend it, and I feel the warm breath from their nostrils. Several will lick as much of my arm as I'll allow. I allow it all. One, whether due to her personality or the texture of her tongue, leaves red, raw splotches on my skin that, depending on her vigor, can last an entire day.

Number 3214 is the one I look for. She's not the softest or the sleekest. She doesn't have the biggest eyes. On the bridge of her forehead, where most of the cows have black fur, she has a thick swirl of dirty white. She is bony, and her coat has lost its shine. But isn't it always the case that we can't help but love those who seem to love us? I make this bold claim because 3214—Fourteen, for short—recognizes me, or so it seems. She moves to the front of the herd deliberately and looks right at me, as if trying to hold eye contact.

I should disclose that my divorce became final during the third week of the shelter-in-place order—the same week I quarantined a feverish bonus-daughter in my basement, just seven days after I'd driven from Saint Paul to Philadelphia and then on to Manhattan to scoop up two college kids. My attorney's email simply said: "You are officially divorced. Please see the attached filed documents for your records." I mention all of this because it's possible if your divorce were finalized during a pandemic, even a necessary and humane divorce, and if you realized for the first time in your adult life you were truly partnerless—this as couples you knew did puzzles together and took walks together and cooked lamb together and had sex and movie marathons and fights together—under these circumstances it's possible you might misread a cow's expression.

But I don't think I have.

Fourteen's dark black eyes focus on mine, and she sticks her big head through the gate, shoving the other cows' heads out of the way. When she's arching her neck to maintain eye contact, the stretch causes her eyeballs to bulge and roll back so that three-quarters of the whites are exposed and only a sliver of cornea. This makes her appear scary and out of her mind, but she is neither. I let her sniff my hand. Then I pet her nose and forehead. The other cows give up, which allows her more room. Eventually she pushes her head all the way through the bars so I can pat the side of her face. She leans heavily into my hand.

I say to her: "Hello, Fourteen. Hello, sweetie. Thanks for saying hi. You like my hand on your face? Yes, you do. Hello, hello."

Since the dying began and the loneliness washed in, people in Iceland have started hugging trees. Paths are cleared so those who can't hug a human can embrace a tree. According to an Icelandic forest ranger, "When you hug [a tree], you feel it first in your toes and then up your legs and into your chest and then up into your head."

In the photos that accompany the article, a man hugging a tree looks *very* into it—a whole-body embrace of a large trunk. Another gentleman has his arms around the tree, but only his fingertips touch the bark. A woman weaves her body in and out of branches with joy. In a separate photo she kisses the tips of the buds like she means it.

Are many of us now experiencing some small semblance of what it feels like to live in a cage: The physical separation from loved ones and the world? The lack of touch? It's an unfair comparison. Still, the solitude causes (or reveals) a gaping feeling in my chest. Is this the way the body holds isolation? How impossible it is for a person to carry the totality of all that is not present.

Leo and his ex are friendly now, two teenagers quarantined together. One of my students is newly in love and, I hear, in good spirits despite the lockdown. My neighbor to the south allows one visitor to her home. He wears a bandana over his long hair, and when he leaves her house across the street, he waves to me and shouts, "Hey, have a good one!"

The last two times I've visited the cows, Fourteen hasn't bothered to get up from the back of the pen. At first I think she's gone, though I can't imagine where she'd go or why. I feel a small tinge of panic. Eventually I see her there, just chilling. She's over me, I guess. I begin looking to develop a new attachment with another cow.

Comedian Ali Sultan says, "A fun activity for couples quarantined together is to go to the park and run in opposite directions."

"Ha ha," I say when I read this. "Hahahahahaha."

Photos by photographers who are sheltering in place keep showing up on my screens. "In this unnatural state of isolation," a *New York Times* article says, "photographers show the things that bind." One image is of a woman standing behind a sheer curtain in a bedroom, looking out the window in the soft morning light. There's a bed behind her, and I can see wrinkled sheets, an embroidered pillowcase. I assume she is the photographer's partner, and I envy the connection between these two people, one of whom saw the other in that light by that window and captured her image. But when I read the text, I discover it is a self-portrait. The photographer, a war correspondent, is sheltering alone. She doesn't mind being alone, she says. She was raised by a single mother, a parasitologist who taught her to be grateful for the smallest things.

Fourteen is hot and cold. One day she's into me; the next she can't be bothered, so happily is she licking a board inside her trough. She attends to the board so vigorously it rattles the metal.

The other cows see it, and yes, they want some of that action, but no, she will not share.

One of my friends, who hears a lot about the cows, sends me piles of temporary tattoos so I can decorate myself with wildflowers. It's a lovely gift, but it's also possible that she wants to change the subject.

Another calf, number thirty-seven, stands back from the gate. She watches but does not move forward. Thirty-seven is special, though it's taken me some time to realize it. When

I visit at night, and all the cows are asleep, and the Icelanders have stopped hugging their trees, and even the new moon and Venus are social distancing, she is the sole cow standing. She has the world to herself, whether she wants it that way or not. She stares straight at me, and I stare back.

I've found another photographer online whose images look the way the inside of my chest feels: Empty streets in fog. A house with just one light on. Wide-open skies under which nothing moves. Footprints in the snow heading toward a house. ("I'll meet you at the window," the photographer's caption says.) A single streetlight shining on a parked car. "Another lonely night in quarantine," is the caption on that one. I read the comments below it:

Damn. That light.

Very silent.

All of a sudden, I miss everyone.

What will happen next? It feels like this planet is a car that has just screeched to a halt, and we've been thrown forward by the sudden braking. By instinct we fling our arms out to stop other people from flying through the windshield, even while their arms are flinging out to stop us. And after the car has stopped, we all look around to see who is still here, who is injured and bleeding. The children are safe. The light outside has changed. Is someone missing from the car? *Is someone missing from the car?*

Some days I cry over everything. I cry over the parade of elementary school teachers in their cars, wearing masks and honking to their students, who are standing on the street corners and also wearing masks. I cry for a friend who has lost family. I cry over the way my now-home, healthy son dances while he eats cereal. Over the other son's sketch of a boy staring at a computer while the pandemic rages in his periphery. Over a gray painting of Saint Paul trains going nowhere in the snow. And for my students, people in cages who've lived disconnected, isolated lives for decades.

Someday the world will spin again. What will we do when the shock wears off and the debris is cleared? A friend who also teaches in prison says that when she returns to class, she will sneak in flower seeds: a tiny act of rebellion. How many wild columbine seeds could she slip under her pinky nail? How many lupine seeds would fit inside the cap of her pen? It would do nothing to free her students from their cages or loneliness, but it would whisper: *I have not forgotten you.*

For my part, I plan to pull the car over at every opportunity and say, "Want in?" I will throw the doors open to my people—both those I've long known are mine and those who still could be. I am realizing I will need a bigger car, maybe a whole damn camper, yet somehow, I believe this can happen. And maybe, once everyone is inside, we will hug each other *and* some trees, because this is my dream and, besides, we're not here long, and the cows would approve. I will talk to the people inside my camper: *Hello, sweetie,* I will say. *Thanks for saying hi. You like my hand on your face? Yes, you do. Hello, hello.*

A few nights ago, in bed, I craved the weight of exactly one human hand on my lower back. It refused to materialize, so I got up and took Toby for a walk. It was late, and I walked and walked down the empty streets toward the cows. Thirty-seven was also awake, standing alone in the barn while the other cows slept. The sight of that insomniac calf brought me inexplicable comfort. I took her photo and sent it to a few friends, all of whom had seen pictures of this same cow before, standing oddly awake in the orange light. From the houses where they were sheltering, a few kind friends, still up and phone-addicted, responded immediately, as if they'd been waiting all week for another image of the strange, sleepless cow. On the walk home Toby rubbed his head against my thigh, and I snapped a photo of the moon.

Music in the Midway

I HEARD HIM BEFORE I saw him. Ron rested a boom box on his left shoulder and whacked oncoming cars with his free hand. He favors the dead center of the road so he can reach both east and westbound traffic. A white guy, all forehead, Ron is in his late fifties, around six-foot tall, one hundred and twenty pounds with shoes on. What he lacks in heft, he makes up for in volume. If he is outside, I hear him, because not only is his boom box blaring Aretha Franklin, his voice rings with rage. *People need to slow the fuck down!* he shouts, walking up to an oncoming car and banging the window. At first, he sounds angry, but listen long enough and you hear the panic build. The disbelief sounds lonely. It sounds like: *Doesn't anyone else see this? How can you all not see this?*

You're going to kill someone! he screams when he approaches a car that's slowing down, trying to drive around him. *Don't you people give a shit?* His tone—raw-throat alarm—unsettles even more than his volume. It says something is urgent and no one is doing a thing about it. *You whore!* he shouts to me, and most women on the block. *You are anti-Black! I can tell by the jeans you're wearing!* A few neighbors reroute their walking path, so they don't have to face him. *Slavery should not have happened!* Beneath his urgency, there's fatigue. *Stop following me,* he tells me when he sees me outside. *I know you're following me.*

A neighbor who knows Ron from his previous placement posts on the neighborhood Facebook group: "Our disabled and mentally ill neighbors are safer in their community when they are known by their neighbors. He is mentally ill and may require de-escalation if agitated. If he's being a danger to himself or others please call 988."

Since he moved into the group home eight months ago, cops have become a constant on my street. *Go home, Ron-Ron,* the cop with the sandy blonde hair says, arms crossed. *Go now.* When the cop tells him to head home, he always does. Ron stops shouting, walks west, away from the squad car. He even turns his music off.

* * *

I moved to this bungalow post-divorce, post-empty-nest. My new neighborhood is called Midway, because it's between downtown Saint Paul and downtown Minneapolis. It's a small neighborhood—grid streets bordered by rail yards, a rock quarry, an industrial park. Within those borders are 1920s Sears starter homes, a coffee shop, some of the city's best Somali and Korean restaurants, and ample big-box stores. I needed something small, affordable, cozy. I want my sons to think of it as "our house," not "Mom's house," but it's not their childhood home. That house, where their dad remained with his new wife, is not quite right either. I project my restlessness: too hot, too cold, too hard, too soft.

Our old place had more trees, less traffic. Though it's

only a few miles down the road, I could swear the light looks different in my new neighborhood. A fellow I'm dating is a landscape artist who paints *en plein air*, which means he's a chaser of sun and shadow. I ask him about my perception of light in Midway. Am I imagining it? Is it the density of homes? The tree-to-asphalt ratio? He says, in his professional experience, light does not shine on landlords or Walmarts, so maybe that explains it.

* * *

Once each year, a nearby private college invites community members to talk about their work in and around the criminal legal system. It's always an uneasy fit for me. Students at this college are required to understand "the carceral geography" to earn their degree in American Studies. Discussions among community activists can become heated, because we have different ideas about the best way to make change. One man suggests that bringing art into the prison gives the carceral behemoth cover for the harm it causes. Others say it's cruel to leave people inside with nothing positive while we wait for the system to change. The discussions start off congenial, but often end on a brittle note. How are we supposed to solve large systemic problems when our own work creates internal friction?

Throughout the years, I'll have similar conversations with students in another class in a wood-paneled room tucked inside a concrete building on the sprawling grounds of a prison that was once a state mental hospital, and before that,

"Minnesota Experimental School for the Feeble Minded." This building and the land beneath it has long been a repository for Minnesota's mass discarding. It's here that I work with writers who are compiling and editing an anthology on precarity in America. The ghosts of past inhabitants sit behind us while students read submissions from struggling others: artists, immigrants, delivery drivers.

CF, one of the editors, says, "Why the fuck aren't we making a book about revolution?" Someone else says, "What on earth makes you think we aren't?" At the heart of this four-year project lurks the question: Where is the safety net for those who need it most?

In prison classrooms and in college classrooms, we read books, and make books, and discuss change with words. Too quiet, too loud, too timid, too narrow.

As hard as that gets, words are the easy part.

Dealing with each other day after day—our friends, our colleagues, our coworkers—that's altogether trickier. Even in the arts, even in nonprofits, people are canceled, people cry, people quit. Social media, the great chorus of exhortation and anger, may platform many good people's highest ideals, but it's so loud as to dilute anything meaningful. Life off the internet seems to mimic what we've built onscreen, and I am not exempt. I'm ever-willing to rage about one person's approach over another's, this org's ethos versus that one's. During one classroom visit I hear myself arguing with an outside activist that they shouldn't criticize without "putting boots on the ground" in the facilities. I leave embarrassed that I used such bullshit language, that I fall into binary thinking when the opposite is required.

Outside of classrooms, it's even more complicated. When difficulty knocks on my literal door, I freeze.

* * *

It's eleven o'clock at night at the end of a long workday. Ron runs door-to-door, banging like he's fleeing fire, boom box vibrating on his shoulder. Someone, four houses down and across the street from me, answers. Ron hollers at the man who steps outside in boxers and bare feet. Ron looks like he's about to whack him, though I don't think he would. The man, on the other hand, who knows? Would he shove him? Is there a gun on his radiator just inside the door?

There's yelling. Staccato yelling. Arms flying. It's getting worse, growing louder.

I do not want to call 911.

Growing up as a latchkey kid, I had only one rule: Call 911 if something bad happens. The nine, the one, the one carved riverbeds in my brain that exist still today. Adrenaline knows exactly what buttons to push.

I'm no longer a kid, and it's clear to me and many others—we need new neural pathways, new rivers. My friend Erin told me before she agreed to work in the prisons that she was an abolitionist. That was a decade ago. She's the first person I met who identified in that way, but she comes from a long line of folks who've done police and prison abolitionist work, steadfast and with hope for most of their lives. The night after George Floyd was murdered, I sat with friends, masked in a parking lot as helicopters filled the sky. We saw smoke. Heard sirens. The uprising had begun.

Can you hear us now?, spray-painted across the Twin Cities.

I asked Erin how it felt to see so many white people joining the protests against police brutality. She said it felt good to have more help. "We're tired."

Years later, after living in the Twin Cities and working in this state's prisons, I understand better why Erin is an abolitionist. I'm new and learning, tentative and overwhelmed.

A few men I've worked closely with—kind, compassionate men who care deeply for others—are locked up because of mental health crises that they did not ask for and for which they've received no help. I think of them when I see a cop car pull up to Ron, whose voice grows louder right this minute, at eleven o'clock at night outside my house.

He and the man in boxers continue to yell, continue to fling arms toward each other.

I call 988, the non-emergency line.

"I'm sorry you're experiencing this," the soft and calm voice on the line says. "Would you like to talk about it?"

"No, I'm calling to get help for a neighbor," I tell the operator.

"Could you put him on the phone?"

"There's no way he's able," I explain.

"I'm sorry," she tells me. "You'll need to call 911."

I step onto my porch in my pajamas, with what plan, I have no idea. Ron turns when he sees my porch light come on. Later, I'll think about my students. I'll think about our discussions of failed systems and change and better solutions. I'll think about visits to college students who must study mass incarceration to get a degree in American Studies. I'll think about the buildings we collectively imagine emptied and the grace those imaginative conversations take. I will think of all of that, but not till later. In the moment, Ron moves toward me, yelling. *You're trying to kill me.* We make eye contact as he reaches my sidewalk, as I step inside. When he begins pounding on my door—*you cunt, stop following me*—I call 911.

* * *

The neighborhood is loud and getting louder. Bach's Brandenburg Concerto No. 1 in F major blares through the night until sunrise, and this music is not coming from Ron's boom box. No one knows what is happening. A man posts a video taken from inside his home. His camera scans the tops of roofs in the dark of night, as the music changes. "It's opera," he says with disbelief. The streetlights flicker in fog. The music echoes. The opera singer's mezzo-soprano pierces the night sky. She sings the song "Flower Duet" from the first act of the opera *Lakmé,* in French. The man who is recording whispers with a small, incredulous laugh, "It's so surreal."

* * *

With warmer weather, Ron is outside daily—sunglasses on, blazer rolled at the sleeves—which means more neighbors are newly and daily christened *whores* and *bigots* and *cunts,* which means the neighborhood Facebook group has become more active on the subject of Ron and how/if/when to help neighbors who struggle with mental illness and how/if/when to protect one another. One neighbor asks for compassion. Ron did well in his old neighborhood and has a history of trying to help out by sweeping sidewalks, the man says.

If you want to see America struggle with transformative justice or the lack thereof, join any neighborhood Facebook group. Ours, regarding Ron:

- "He has been blocking cars. If you try to move, he runs in front of you or hits/kicks the car."
- "He has blocked children from riding their bicycles down the sidewalk."
- "I wish it were as simple and black-and-white but his behavior is erratic."
- "He was in my neighbor's face calling her a 'woman thing.' I did not like that. She is family to me."
- "I've had and seen really good results de-escalating agitated folks in camps by offering a cigarette."
- "Just stand back when he does get out of control and let the spirits take care of it."

* * *

I wonder if our neighborhood could form a response group instead of calling the cops. Someone suggests I ask the folks at the Department of Safety and Inspections (DSI) to get better information about Ron. I call the agent for Ramsey

County. The DSI agent claims they have received an average of two to three calls per day about Ron for the last several months. He has guardians who aren't taking an interest, she says, in an accusatory tone. A neighborhood interventionist group, she tells me, is not a good idea for a few reasons, one of which is that a police response signals to Ron that he needs to "make better choices."

"He is mentally ill," I say.

"Yes, but he still needs to make better choices," she tells me.

This is surely what Ibram X. Kendi means when he says, "Americans have long been trained to see the deficiencies of people rather than policy."

DSI's policy, she tells me, dictates that they can't file charges against Ron for disorderly conduct until someone fills out a form for citizen's arrest, and until that happens it will remain a civil issue, not a criminal issue. Arresting Ron is what I'd hoped to avoid, I tell her. As if she doesn't really have a box for that option, she doubles down: No one wants to be that person, she tells me. But? *If just one person would sign it?* Then we could file charges.

* * *

The week after my call, DSI sends me two letters, with photos included. They need me to trim the lilac bush that overhangs my sidewalk within four days, or they will charge me $250.00 per hour for labor. It's the only blooming thing on my property.

* * *

We hear it blare into the night—"Flower Duet," featuring the daughter of a Brahmin priest and her servant who gather flowers along the river. Translated, these words pierce the night sky in mezzo-soprano:

> By flower banks, fresh and bright,
> On the flow'rd bank, gay in morning light,
>
> Come, and join we their meeting.
> Come, and join we their meeting.

* * *

Folks call 911, each other, the non-emergency line, the Department of Safety and Inspections, and countless other numbers to say: There is music so loud we cannot sleep, and we have no idea where it is coming from. We are so many people living among each other, and we are so poorly equipped to handle our collective problems. DSI and 911 do not help. *Ron is harassing me! The music is wild! He called me a cunt. Someone please tell us where the music is coming from?! I've slept eight hours in three days.*

* * *

"Get your ass to your side of the street right this second," I hear someone yell. I am inside wiping the counters. "And *do not talk to her like that again,* or I swear to god I'll knock you on your ass."

"You people have no idea," Ron yells by way of defense.

I walk into the backyard and listen to the yelling, prepared to do . . . what? Like a character from a B-rate movie, the man keeps yelling: "One more time! Say it one more time, motherfucker, and I swear to god!"

When the man's voice sounds like it is about to shatter, Ron leaves, and the man stops threatening.

Since their fight, the silence has been audible.

Since their fight, Ron has disappeared.

* * *

"Ron's in jail," my neighbor tells me the next time I see her pruning something. She sets her tools down, and gestures in the direction of the house he's not currently sleeping in. Her response lands somewhere between resigned and unsurprised. The quiet makes sense now. His loudest episodes were always followed by a silence, that I assumed meant Ron was inside, laying low.

Someone must have filled out the form.

* * *

Punishment is America's default, our culturally inherited impulse, our great dead end. The United States currently has over seven thousand prisons, jails, and detention centers that hold more than two million people. We stuff them beyond capacity. Activist-philosopher Angela Davis tells us we must "act as if it's possible to change the world and . . . to do it all the time." But what is the alternative? What if we decide we will no longer fill cells with real people? Abolitionists imagine. Imagining is one thing, but *asserting* your ideas feels intimidating: for fear of looking naïve, saying or doing or seeing something the wrong way. Offending someone. Or failing. (A student I work with points out the carceral state is already a proven failure on recidivism rates alone and wonders how could we possibly do worse.) It's scary to think of getting called out, canceled, or even owning my confusion.

I don't want to contribute to the culture that makes trying feel scary.

* * *

Artist Matthew Christopher doesn't envision empty prisons, he photographs them. His photographs are, among many things, a study in the aesthetics of disposability. Rust accumulates across bars that once held men. In stark contrast and at the same time, moss climbs walls, blanketing them a plush green. It's not the case that the people in this now-emptied space were sent back to the community in favor of more effective rehabilitation. Quite the contrary. The cells are empty because we needed bigger buildings to hold more men.

What's possible in a space that once caged humans? If we combined Davis's exhortation with Christopher's photos: Trees rise up in fallow yards. Weeds wind up the ceiling-high windows of now-empty cells. Or it becomes one of countless prison museums—one for each state, so our descendants and theirs can see the spot at Stillwater Prison, B West, Cell 214, where countless real people were caged, one at a time, over the course of a century. Or perhaps, more practically and less poetically, we interrupt cycles of harm and punishment by filling those empty buildings with social services the folks who once lived in them lacked. Instead of Minnesota Correctional Facility Rush City: Minnesota Center for Food. Center for Mental Health. Center for Recovery. Center for Housing Neighbors.

* * *

The screaming opera, we learn, comes from an anti-loitering noise machine. The owners of the local strip mall don't want people sleeping in their parking lot. Far from being apologetic, the property manager is proud people are no longer camping on their sidewalks at night, she says, outside the emptied Herberger's store, just across the parking lot from At Home, which contains velvet throw pillows in every color. Aisles for miles in every hue of blue, purple, gray, green, teal, emerald, rust, scarlet, red. A neighbor posts the property manager's personal cell phone number and urges all the tired neighbors to call her. People call.

* * *

Ron is being evicted. *They're kicking me out!* he yells at everyone who walks by. *I'm going to live on the streets!*

He sees me while I'm walking Toby and stops me by saying: "STOP! Do not move a muscle!"

I stand entirely still.

"If you are a fucking adult, you should understand what I'm asking of you!"

I stand as unmoving as I humanly can. Toby sighs and lays down beside my feet.

"I'm being evicted in one month," Ron says.

"I'm sorry, Ron. Do you have another place to go?" I imagine him stuck outside the At Home store, him on the concrete just a few feet from aisles overflowing with velvet pillows and "hotel scent" candles.

"What the fuck kind of response is that?!" Ron yells. "I tell you I'm being evicted and that's what you say?"

* * *

The property manager disconnects her cell phone number and is no longer reachable. She was not arrested, of course, nor charged or threatened with disorderly conduct, nor fined. And the people who slept on sidewalks will keep moving along, but to where?

* * *

adrienne maree brown asserts it's the way we live our daily lives, with our neighbors, friends, and kin, that build our transformative justice muscles. We can't, in other words, stop sending our neighbors to prison and envision flourishing alternatives until we interrogate the ways we wield punishment in our own lives. This pokes at some deep reluctance in me. Reckonings with those I'm closest to are the hardest—harder than calling DSI or a non-emergency line, harder than talking with new neighbors to information share, and harder, certainly, than classroom discussions or even making a book about all of the above. My defaults—silence, retreat, sometimes gossip—are a form of punishment, not an impulse to repair.

"People mess up," brown says in her book *We Will Not Cancel Us: And Other Dreams of Transformative Justice*. "We lie, exaggerate, hurt, and abandon each other. When we hear that something bad has happened, it makes sense to feel anger, pain, confusion, and sadness. But to move immediately to punishment means that we stay on the surface of what has happened."

I've often enacted, in other words, *carceral logic*—sever, dispose, punish—with people in my daily life, in my very circle, without realizing I was doing so. I could stand to learn candor over silence. I could spend more time imagining forgiveness and less time nursing hurts.

brown notes that we have a reflexive tendency toward "mass and intimate punishments." She's talking about internet callouts and public cancellations, and there's all of that—the social media screaming, all the ways we forget that those closest to us are quite often the closest to also caring about what matters most to us. The way we measure each other's technique, commitment, visionary failings, and shortfalls—but also the infinitesimal cancellations we enact in our lives on a daily basis.

Can we unlearn this?

I am living in this new neighborhood because I'm newly

divorced from a man who claimed I could hold a grudge for a lifetime. We were good to each other for so long, and then we weren't. I'm not suggesting it's only my fault our marriage ended, or even that it should've been saved, but I do wonder how differently things might have looked—in that relationship and many others in my life—if I had asked for repair earlier and more often, instead of shutting people out.

Isn't the answer always closest to home?

It's among our own people that the muscle memory of our moral imagining is built. The same is true for problem-solving, and our forgiveness. It's the lifetime of hourly, humble, unsexy, hard-fought interactions with those closest to us, closer even than your neighbor three houses down, that usher change.

"When we face pain in relationships," bell hooks notes, "our first response is often to sever bonds rather than to maintain commitment."

I do, in fact, wish to sever bonds. All the time.

After fourteen years in this city, a decade longer than any other community, I both crave community and feel an itch to flee: to the desert, to a cabin in the woods. It's not Ron's yelling and it's not the midnight operas. It's hurtful comments that I never address, which fester. It's others' silence about my own harms that I never question. It's unaddressed wrongs that I refuse to confront, or once confronted, cannot forgive. Abolition is presence, not absence, Ruth Wilson Gilmore says. Presence is hard because staying is hard.

* * *

Ron has been evicted. It happened after his detention in County. He refuses to move, so it will take time and lawyers before it's settled, before neighbors stop hearing his frightened yells. A few months ago, one of the many times the police showed up threatening arrest, he hollered, *If you kick me out I'll be homeless! I'll live on the streets!* This was before the opera music blared into Midway's night skies, after Ron's Aretha Franklin.

Today he is leaning out of his upstairs window—fully, half of his long body talking to the sky. I hear music coming from his room.

"I'm a big fan of women!" he says.

"Hi, Ron." I wave.

"Ma'am, ma'am! Stop right there. I am talking to you! STOP. Is it true or is it not," he says, "that the entire Saint Paul city council has been invaded by women?"

"It is true," I say.

"Now I have a question for you. I've lived in this goddamn neighborhood for eight months and the cops tell me 'yes' and 'no' at the same time. I ask you: Is it possible to mean yes and no at the same time?"

"No," I say, for the sake of argument. "They have to choose."

He smiles. "Thank you. That's all I fucking wanted to know. I'm coming outside. Do not move."

He disappears from the window. One second later, he opens the front door and steps onto the porch.

"I like your dog," he says, of my shiny mutt.

"His name is Toby."

"Toby has great sheen," Ron says. "I'm a big fan of sheen."

He takes one step toward me. "I only have one friend on this entire goddamn street and her name is Kate, the same name as yours." He points to a woman across the street who is sitting on her porch smoking, but who does not wave back.

"My name is actually Jen," I tell him, not for the first time.

He smiles at me for one second, nods in approval. "Jenny. I know where you live," he says, and he points in the direction of my house.

He's almost smiling, and I think I'm getting better at talking with Ron, and I feel relieved, maybe even hopeful, but just for a minute.

"Yes, that's right," I say, trying to hold eye contact. Trying to make connection. Trying to do better than fail him again. His smile fades and he yells, "Stop fucking staring at me, goddamn it!" He calls me a bitch.

That's my cue to go. I turn away, but before I'm even one house distant, he starts again. "Hey! Answer one question for me. DOES MY MUSIC DISTURB YOUR PEACE? Asshole! Get back here when I'm talking to you! I asked you a question! I asked if my music is disturbing your peace!"

I stop. I turn to Ron. Too hot, too cold, too hard, too soft. Too direct, too demure, too cynical, too naive. Maybe the only good answer is to keep trying.

"I don't like the names you call me," I say. "But, I do like your music."

He cranks his radio, and I turn, again, toward home. "You've never volunteered a day in your goddamn life!" he says. A car drives past, too fast for this road. "You choose to walk on the left side of the street because you're a coward! Hey, Kate, turn around and look at me when I'm talking to you!"

He keeps yelling. I keep walking.

Soon he'll be gone, and someone new will move into his room—top left, window wide open, bugs be damned.

Don't you give a shit? he yells.

Don't any of you people give a shit?!

People need to *slow the fuck down!*

Aretha Franklin belts "Ain't No Mountain High Enough" from Ron's boom box and he yells, *Fucking fuck off!* at me, or his group home, or Midway, or this entire country, then he pauses, legs bent, back arched, head to sky, and he sings harder than I've heard him—not at peace, exactly, but finding respite in the song—loud, then louder, leaning into the wail.

Surrogates

"That anyone loves us at all is not a given."

—HANIF ABDURRAQIB

1.

PETS FLOATED AWAY FROM their owners after Hurricane Katrina, leaving the streets awash in orphaned animals. In response, a shelter sprang up inside Louisiana's Dixon Correctional Institute. Housing pets in prison worked so well that the state made the shelter permanent. That's how, long after the disaster, eleven incarcerated men became caretakers to ninety animals, and one of those animals became mine.

Once each year this shelter brings dogs to an adoption event at the Angola Prison Rodeo. Outside an arena where men wearing black-and-white stripes are bludgeoned by bulls, stray dogs bark from crates. Spectators who wish to adopt may trial-walk puppies on leashes alongside men who will never go home again.

Almost a decade ago, I passed through that puppy yard on my way to an interview. I overheard someone say in a sweet Southern drawl, "It's her fourth Angola rodeo. Poor girl."

Poor girl lay sprawled in her kennel, a skinny, despondent dog with the face of a greyhound, the body of a Lab, and the neck of a giraffe. Her name was Twin, and she wouldn't make eye contact or raise her head for anyone but Wyatt, her assigned caretaker. I overheard Wyatt say, "We've had her over four years. I don't know why no one wants her. She's going to make someone the nicest pet." It's the way he said *nicest pet*—soft and grave, like he really meant it—that registered.

Nearby, vendors hawked food, children jabbered, dogs yipped—and incarcerated men ran from bulls to become the "winner," which is to say, the last man crushed, because in this rodeo, imprisoned men are both sport and prop. Because I teach in prison, each time a man was whacked into the fence (applause!), I thought of specific people from my classroom who I know well, people whose stories I've read, people whose words, written in pencil, sometimes describe being a kid no one wanted.

"Real gentle girl," Wyatt said at the same time the announcer whooped and the crowd cheered about another "pin" down. My anger spiked. Adopting Twin felt like saying *Screw you* to discarding. Twenty-five bucks and a signature later, she was mine.

Later came her side-eyed avoidance, her vile breath, her terror. This new friend took days to come out of the crate, a month to housebreak, to eat a full bowl of food, to lean into my leg, to look at me.

A year after I brought Twin home, I called the prison to speak to Wyatt. I wanted to tell him he was right: She did make the nicest pet. First I had to speak to the administrator overseeing the dog-rescue program, who asked in a thick Southern accent, "*Wyatt*? Why on earth would you want to talk to Wyatt? He's a retard, ain't you, Wyatt?" Wyatt was in the office, waiting for my call. Over the man's chuckling, I heard Wyatt respond, but I couldn't make out his words. "He don't know nothing about *nothing*," the officer said.

When he finally handed the phone over, I told Wyatt that Twin's favorite spot was anyone's lap. When I grabbed her leash, she spun in a circle then sat eagerly in front of me, locking eyes and politely putting one paw on my thigh. She would share a treat or her food, but she did not like sharing affection; when others came around, Twin stretched out her paws to block them from my lap, and groaned this long, guttural sound that seemed to mean, "Please, *mine*."

Wyatt laughed and said that sounded right. Twin had lived inside a concrete kennel for four of her five years. Wyatt, who also lived inside a concrete box, had gone to prison as a teen. He'd cared for Twin since she was a puppy, which meant he had likely opened her kennel to feed her and let her out thousands of times. I pictured him petting her and saying, "Hey, girl," every single time he opened her door. Among the slamming of cages and barking of other dogs, it must've been a comfort for her. And for him.

She refused to walk with me the day I met her in that muddy yard, but as soon as Wyatt took the leash, she trotted willingly. He leaned down and spoke to her after I signed all the paperwork. He talked to her for a long while, her body resting against his legs.

Before we hung up, I asked Wyatt what his plans were when he got out. Quietly, he said he'd been thinking about creating his own organization that would teach other prisons how to take in strays and "treat them right."

I'd had Twin for four years when she grew listless, and her breathing turned wheezy. She coughed a lot, and her black nose dripped. Her affection remained intact, however, which is why I figured it was just a cold and waited almost two weeks to take her to the vet. (Maybe also because I was in the middle of a divorce, with full custody of my kids, while working fifty hours a week.)

The vet told my soon-to-be-ex-husband and me it was fungal pneumonia, which, at this stage, had a 10 percent chance of responding to the medication. Twin, who was terrified in the tiny kennel, and terrified in general of anyone who wasn't family, would need to continue to stay in the hospital during the treatment, and the final bill would be around $10,000. Did we want to treat or euthanize her?

I don't know why I didn't research it. I don't know why I didn't ask for a day to think about it. Was I too overwhelmed to think clearly?

Even after all these years, I don't want to tell you what we decided. I think it was the wrong choice. I asked Twin if she wanted to go for one last walk, and she perked up as if we were leaving the hospital and going home to her couch. She trotted outside alongside me and leaned in as if all her troubles were gone. As if she were safe.

2.

Al joined our family the day he married my mother. We have one photo from the wedding, a Polaroid: He stands six feet, seven inches tall, shirtless, with a pink carnation tucked in his chest hair. A foot shorter and to his left, Mom wears a brown cotton dress and a matching flower in her hair. At five years old I stand between my two sisters, Marie (older) and Kathleen (younger), all of us wearing matching pink dresses and white bobby socks. We're posing in front of what is possibly the only tree in Muleshoe, Texas.

That night, and many nights after, Al let me stand on his size thirteen cowboy boots and dance the two-step to Kenny Rogers. Less than six months later he forced me to eat a whole box of cookies because I had whined for another. Cookie dust mixed with tears and snot as I ate my punishment. My sisters, unable to help, watched quietly. After I finished the container, Al hugged me and said, "Love ya, Baby."

The names he called me changed with his mood: Jenner, Liar, Sissy, Chickenshit, Asshole, Baby Doll, Dumb Shit, Thunder Thighs, Squirt.

In the first year Al was a part of our family, I two-stepped through the air, weightless; I rode a bike while Al pushed; I sprinted past closets, scared of the dark; I was crying, always crying, but I never knew why.

He gave big, wraparound hugs. He pushed us into walls. He bruised our bare thighs with his belt. He baked cobbler using peaches he'd picked from our tree. He would later call my sister's boyfriend Hard Dick or Numb Nuts or Dumb

Fuck. Some of his name-calling was ridiculous enough to make you laugh—unless he screamed it, in which case you ran. His anger was a fierce wind, surging at unpredictable times from traumas I never learned.

You wanted to be around him, and you wanted to flee him. We had a visiting squirrel one year, entirely because of Al. He trained the squirrel to come running along the top of the fence when he tapped two pecans together. He trained the squirrel to take the pecan from his outstretched hand. He even trained that squirrel—and I watched him do it—to scurry into our open living room, walk up his leg, and accept a pecan from his palm while standing on his bare chest.

That was the same spring Al planted seeds that made orange and yellow marigolds grow beneath the mailbox, even though our house was just a rental. He tended the marigolds. He remarked on all six of them most times when we pulled into the driveway as if their very existence was a miracle. As it was. Flowers from nothing.

"I love you," he said daily. And also, "I don't give a goddamn hell if Jesus Christ himself is sitting on the dashboard of this goddamn car, I'm not going through the drive-in / turning up the heater / changing the channel / turning around."

Al mostly stopped parenting his own four children after he married my mom. During an unprecedented weekend when Al's kids visited, he scrambled eggs while we sat stiffly and stared at bodybuilders on TV. As he cooked, I asked him to sign a permission slip for school.

He took the slip from my hand, read it, and gave me a confused look. "Why would I sign this?" He said it like he truly did not understand. The six children sitting awkwardly in the living room turned from the TV to watch us.

"I need a parent's signature," I said.

He put the spatula down and stared at me. He paused with great deliberation. Somehow I knew what was coming.

"I'm not your parent," he said.

Al had been married to Mom for about ten years by this point. He'd coached my basketball team, danced with me, hugged me before bed, came to my school plays. Now he handed back the unsigned permission form, and would not look away, as if his ability to face me were proof that what he'd said were true.

Decades later, when Al was dying, I traveled down Highway 60 to say goodbye. Corn husks blew across the road and combines harvested into the night. My body felt the memory of being a small child dancing for the first time on someone else's boots, to someone else's rhythm. I was in both bodies at once: a five-year-old on Al's feet, an adult driving a car.

I'm glad that was the memory my body chose.

When I walked into his room, Al cried out from the bed and reached for me like a child. Surprised, I looked to my sisters for confirmation of what I was seeing. I wondered if it was the morphine doing all that caring, and I chose not to mind if it was. If there's a gift in certain death, it's a chance to control the ending, which one might confuse with the entire journey if one wanted to. And I did.

Al had endured a severely restricted diet for months, but now that he was in hospice care, he could eat what he wanted, and just then what he wanted was salami sliced so thin you could see through it. "Hear me?" he asked with a grin. He motioned with clumsy hands. "*That thin!*"

I asked the man at the deli to slice the salami like lace. The man, who did not know he was part of a sacred task, adjusted knobs and slid the meat against the spinning blade. When he tossed the first slice onto the scale, it was so thin it did not even register.

I brought it to Al, and he held a slice up to the light, admiring the cut. I'd gotten it right, and he rewarded me with a smile.

We held hands more in his last two days than we had in all our years together. I asked if he was scared, and he said, "Not if you're here."

Who is this man? I wondered. *Who is he confusing me for?*

A few days into my visit, he requested a grilled cheese sandwich—his literal last meal. I placed three different kinds of cheese inside two pieces of Asiago bread and grilled them until the entire house smelled of browned butter. Al said it was the best he'd ever eaten.

"Please, God," he said, folding his hands and pretending to pray, "let me live one more day so I can eat three more."

3.

Charlotte's Web author E. B. White was also someone's stepdad, and by all accounts a devoted one. When I imagine an ideal parent—and I'm ashamed that, after all my own parenting failures, I still imagine an ideal parent—he is E. B. White.

In a letter to the humane society, White responded to accusations that he was harboring an unlicensed dachshund.

"If by 'harboring' you mean getting up two or three times every night to pull Minnie's blanket up over her," he wrote, "I am harboring a dog all right. The blanket keeps slipping off. I suppose you are wondering by now why I don't get her a sweater instead. That's a joke on you. She has a knitted sweater, but she doesn't like to wear it for sleeping."

4.

I was not raised around extended family. Nor did I grow up with a "chosen family," a phrase introduced in 1991, the year I graduated high school, by Kath Weston in the book *Families We Choose: Lesbians, Gays, Kinship*. In making visible the bonds queer people form in the absence of support from their biological families, Weston articulated alternate family models—ways to become, to select, and to name surrogates.

A former student turned friend, brought up in foster care, introduces me to others as his "chosen family." I'm honored that he says it so openly. I have friends who feel like family, but I'm reluctant to name that feeling, especially when they're rich with relatives. Would it feel clingy? Unwelcome? If they agreed, could the relationship withstand the pressure of that title? Such are the doubts of a girl whose chosen dads didn't choose her back, I suppose.

5.

It has been four years since Twin was euthanized. Five years since Al died. I'm solo parenting my own kids, and I doubt I'll ever remarry. Curious, still, about stepfathers in nature, I type into Google, "surrogate fathers animal world." There are six. I try "capable stepfathers animal world," which brings up a list of . . . surrogate *mothers*. There's an orangutan who takes in tiger cubs. A Pomeranian who adopts a monkey. A dog who adopts a squirrel, a cat who adopts a squirrel—really every kind of animal willingly adopts squirrels.

My favorite surrogate of them all is the cat, Lurlene, who takes in a pit bull. A fly-infested, one-day-old puppy whimpered from a garbage can. Some woman brushed him off, named him, and tucked him right up against her cat, Lurlene, who was nursing kittens at the time. Lurlene mewed and fed the puppy along with the rest of her litter. In a photo taken a bit later, the puppy is gazing with milky, three-week-old eyes right into Lurlene's whiskers. There are photos of Lurlene with all her kittens and that starving baby pit bull at her nipples, and their little heads and mouths are all frantic and needy, yet every one of them is being nourished, and Lurlene has this look on her face like, *Good God, let it end*. She doesn't leave the cardboard box, though, or thwack any of them with her paws. She feeds them. Then the kittens grow into cats and the puppy grows into a pit bull and Lurlene gets her nipples back.

6.

My alley-neighbor, Jonathan, has a string of lights in his yard that loop from his detached garage, over the bistro table, and through the trees. He plugs them in when his daughter comes home from college. One night, when the lights were shining, I heard the clink of bottles and smelled a warming grill and heard him joke with his daughter about "little smokies." Anytime I look out my back door and see glimmers between Jonathan's oak leaves, I think a light-worthy someone must be over, and that feels safe to me, and a little special, the way I imagine it does to his guest. It's a habit I've made since I can remember, assuming all the homes that are well lit, with shoveled walks in winter, and planted gardens in July, hold people who are well loved. It can't be that simple, but it's still a comforting thought. Under those trees and lights: a home. I wonder how different the world would be if every human knew that feeling.

7.

Prior to marrying Al, Mom worked two jobs, seven days a week, and still needed government assistance. Would we have had an Al if my mom had lived near family, or if my dad had stuck around post-divorce, or if we'd had our own chosen family? In the absence of a village, Americans sometimes take a spouse—or so it seems. As a single mother, my mom had no choice but to drive us to childcare in pajamas in the wee hours of the morning: My sisters and I spent most of our time in daycare under the care of people who didn't care all that much. The year I entered kindergarten, Marie and I were on our own. Mom left for work at four a.m. and dropped Kathleen off at daycare. Later Marie woke me, dressed me, and walked me to school. I remember butter-and-sugar sandwiches, stomachaches, and a boy who taunted us till Marie scared him off by tossing (someone else's) garden tomatoes at his head. Mostly I remember school picture day.

Mom had rolled my hair in foam curlers the night before, coiling each section until my hair was engulfed by pink sponge. She asked Marie to take the rollers out the next morning and she laid out what I was to wear: a white blouse with puffy sleeves and a maroon ribbon bow tie.

Marie coaxed me awake, then unspooled roller after roller. When I looked in the mirror, I saw a disaster. My hair was rounded, like a salon perm. Like an egoless grandma. My very head had tripled in size. I bawled while Marie tried to brush out the curls, but that only made the helmet fuller. I cried harder. She sprayed my hair and tried to smush it close to my scalp, but helping only hurt.

When it was time to leave for school, Marie laid the brush down, tied my ribbon into a bow, and locked the door behind us.

This was lifetimes ago. My sister and I now have grown kids, and she tells me she is weary of looking after everyone. Marie reminds me she began parenting at the age of seven. She means me, of course. She is ready for a break—fly-to-Mexico-and-never-return ready. I've only lately realized that sometimes trauma doesn't catch up with you until you sit down. My sister has finally sat down.

I haven't seen the school photo in years. It's buried in a box in Mom's garage, tucked away with the picture of the five of us at the tiny Texas wedding, and snapshots of grandfathers I never knew, a father I don't remember, Al standing on red dirt in his big boots, a squirrel on the edge of a fence. Filed away somewhere, with no logic or respect for chronology, is that school photo, with its stock blue background and my eyes, red and puffy. What's not visible is the mother who needed support, and the immeasurable goodwill of the sister who stepped up to fill the void.

8.

My final flock of backyard chickens was the hardest, in part because I'd named them after family. Kathleen was the smallest of the newly added chicks, and she didn't live long enough to lay an egg. Marie survived all the perils, the earliest and bloodiest of which was when my dog (not Twin, but Toby) burst into the coop and hauled the hens out to play. Just as he did with his squeaky toys, he picked them up by the neck and tossed them into the sky. He tussled them—joyful and wild, until they stopped playing.

Of all the motley-feathered pullets that bore my family members' names, only Marie plus the elder hens remained. Three months after the dog attack, Marie suffered a weasel invasion in broad daylight. From inside the house, I heard screeching and fluttering and my neighbor's screams. By the time I could intervene, blood and feathers covered the coop. Several of the newest hens lay dead.

Again, Marie survived. But every time I dumped grain into her trough, she attacked my hand. I wanted to make this right; I'd given the bird my sister's name, after all. Alas, it was too late. Her beak was her defense, and she deployed it with precision. She left welts on my hand anytime I went near. My animal impulse against the pain was to whack Marie's soft, golden feathers. Instead, I sprinkled grain at her feet to show her I wasn't a threat, but even that did not sway her.

One stormy night she wandered out of the coop and couldn't find her way back. The next morning I discovered her wet and huddled under a tree. To my surprise she did not attack me, did not make a single murmur in her gullet when I picked her up. Her delicate bones felt so resigned in my arms that I thought we'd made a breakthrough. Eventually she recovered and made it clear she'd simply been too tired to fight.

There were gentle days, too, of course. Days the chickens pecked beneath a sunny sky and roosted at sundown. Days when the dangers were scarce and the world was well. Whether the transcendent times made up for the brittle moments, I can't say. Either way, the hens aged and stopped laying eggs. With my permission, my neighbor slaughtered Marie and the rest of the flock. I chose not to be there for it, nor to eat the soup she shared with me, including a container of broth made from Marie's bones. It's still in my freezer, golden and frost covered, some seven years later because I can neither use it nor throw it out.

Despite how much I loved their sounds and squalor, that was the last year I kept chickens. I told myself, *Not again.* Who needs that heartbreak in your life? Not just the heartbreak of watching a living thing struggle, but of failing to protect it, too. The grief of failing others is sharper even than being failed. And yes, it's human, and yes, it's inevitable. But that doesn't make it less painful.

I focus so much on all of love's failings, I've forgotten how nice it feels to try. Recently, in honor of my birthday, some friends rented a farmhouse with four squawking chickens and a wraparound porch. They brought homemade hand pies and chocolate cake. We read during the day and chopped vegetables for soup each night. I couldn't wait to bring scraps to the hens. It felt nice to think of each carrot I peeled as a treat for the birds, to offer something that made them squawk and flutter. And, of course, it was a gift to find their eggs in the morning: multi-sized and multicolored, each one cradling a golden yolk. I am warming to the idea of raising chickens again. Just a few. It's easier to support others when you, yourself, feel held.

My friends, who hear often of my neighbor's yard lights, offered to help me string some at my new place. Because I am slower to accept care than I am to talk about it, I haven't said yes, not yet. But if I do, I will hang those lights above a tiny coop, drape them above a circle of chairs, and let them illuminate the renegade sunflower in my small backyard. When my people visit, I will plug the lights in as a sign that they are worthy. That we all are.

Blueprint

My mother is at her most maternal when standing beside a sick person, all the better if he's dying. She's a hospice nurse and a good one. Before she retired, she spent fifty hours a week dosing morphine, checking vitals, helping people die, and telling stories about all of the above. Her voice grows strong when talking about health because she's confident in that way of caring. *Are you dizzy? Yeah? How often are you peeing?* Second-born from a Catholic family of ten, chain-smoker (till she quit), nervous driver, good listener, kind. She has high cheekbones, soft skin, and chestnut eyes—*a looker,* I tell her when she is in her seventies, and I mean it. She did not show affection through physical touch, so as a kid it felt special when she set the newspaper down, held my wrist—two fingers pressed to pulse—to concern herself with the very beat of my heart.

The most reliable way to barter love in my family was to feel sick or take care of someone who was. Which is why I had epilepsy, diabetes, and cancer, all before the age of sixteen, until it was confirmed, after much investigation, that I did not have any of those things. My sister Marie—thyroid. Kathleen—heart. *Something's Not Right* was my mother's mantra. Couple that with *Better to Be Safe Than Sorry* and you have an insurance company's nightmare.

I am six. It's not yet sunrise, and my mother has to leave for work, but first she lays a blanket on top of me. Dust particles float around her as she sets a sleeve of saltine crackers on my lap, lays cool fingers on my forehead. She asks if my stomach hurts and, of course, it does. It's a gnawing. A welling before the tears. She says goodbye in a voice edged with concern. Pre-cell-phone era. Pre-call-your-mom-at-work era. I close my eyes and hear her footsteps walk away. Her keys rattle on the counter. The lighter clicks. I smell smoke. The door shuts—first the wooden door, then the screen. Tires drive through rain on the street outside our door, then silence follows. I am alone, but I do not want to be.

The ache in my stomach is flu, or an ulcer, or maybe longing, a word I don't yet know. Even now, as an adult, when I hear someone say, *I want my mom,* this feeling is what I hear.

* * *

Since my kids came into the world, I worry over how to love right. Or at least, how to love *well.* As if there's a formula, and I'll figure it out by sorting through my own family, my past and present, weighing it all against the rest of the world—like little jerry-rigged case studies using my own shifting methodology.

Like this? Not that? Like her, like him? Like them?

Case Study with Imaginary Illness

Paramedics encircled Al in the kitchen. He'd collapsed—all 350 pounds of him—and my sisters and I broke his fall the best we could. Mom was at work, but we knew the drill for seizures and chest pain. The amber glass bottle of nitroglycerin lived in the side of the refrigerator door and took seconds to locate. But this was the one time his chest pain didn't subside, even after I slipped the white pill under his tongue. He clutched his chest, and his moans grew louder the longer the paramedics worked over him.

Folks from town donated money after the heart attack. Someone took the bills—the fives, tens, twenties—rolled them, tied them in red ribbon, and hung them from the branches of a metal birch tree. The money tree sat on a table behind the couch, and it looked so special, dangling dollars in the air. All that money, all that care, for us.

Except there was no heart attack. This time or during falls that followed.

Angina, at best. But because he was a large man, well, he seemed like someone who *could* have heart trouble, and besides that no one was going to tell him it was all in his head. And no one ever did, not to his face. By the time I was ten, I knew to mistrust Al's stories—in truth, to mistrust most of the words that came out of his mouth—but somehow I exempted his health, which seemed validated by doctors in white coats and the medications that filled our cabinets. It took thirty years before Mom told me his heart attacks weren't real. That the daily vomiting was an eating disorder—not stomach problems. That his seizures weren't epilepsy, but psychogenic non-epileptic seizures. I was an adult with my own healthy kids before I realized my upbringing may have leaned Munchausen-*ish*. Now renamed *factitious disorder*, which stems from anxiety and depression. Check and check.

No doubt someone reading this is saying, *Wait, that's not love. I thought we were studying love?*

It does get confusing, doesn't it?

Case Study with Differential Diagnoses

The appointments came in waves. Tests. Migraines. Meds. Each time my mom underwent a workup, I'd worry about what life would look like if she became debilitated from chronic illness, or worse, died. While we waited for doctors to figure out "what the hell was going on," she remained behind the closed door of her room at the top of the emerald-carpeted hallway, and we knew not to knock.

Case Study with Imaginary Illness and Bonus Differential Diagnoses

A stomach ache from an emotional week sophomore year at another new school resulted in a doctor's appointment, which turned into a prescription, which turned into a rash, which turned into a biopsy, which turned into a referral, which turned into a full blood workup, which led to nurse-Mom insisting to specialist-doctor that *something's not right*, which lead to an extended, cover-your-ass hospital stay. I had maybe-leukemia. That, you can imagine, turned into a confetti drop of care: phone calls from old friends and the boy I adored; a new velvet nightgown with lace on the bottom; a bouquet of gerbera daisies from my friend's mom, whose daughter actually *did have* leukemia, and who bought me this larger-than-normal, vibrant bouquet because she believed I was dying. Like all the other maybe-somethings I had, this also turned out fine.

Years after I left home—grown and raising kids of my own—I learned: I am a healthy person! Not only do I not have diseases or disorders, my immune system is a Ferrari. Yawn.

No one ever consciously invented illness, but sickness was welcomed in the way you'd watch a horror flick. It's going to be scary, but thrilling, too, and you won't do it alone.

Case Study with Cat Family

In what I've come to think of as "the smoking chair," my mom would sit after work and talk about her day to me. In serial form—like Dickens, or *Days of Our Lives,* she told end-of-life stories about real people and their people, about caretaking or its lack.

In the cat family, for example, three daughters sat vigil over their dying father, who did not speak English. They served as his translator, housekeeper, his full-time care. When he died, his daughters insisted on bathing and shaving their father, performing the sacred work the Western world might relegate to an undertaker. What made it tricky, aside from their grief, was the cat that wrapped himself around their father after his last breaths left his body. My mother was taken by the way the daughters bathed him, allowing the cat to stay curled, moving him only when needed to wash their father's neck. Once they were done, they sat vigil—the daughters by his side, the cat beneath his chin, and that's how my mother left them when she said goodbye.

There were stories of narcotics-gone-wrong: folks surrounded by coffee cups and soured towels, fractured bonds, snipping and yelling. A dying mother who cried out in the kind of pain that would drive even sane and sober people to look for an escape. Which folks did, thus the disappearing morphine and the new lockbox—a mini-safe installed to keep family members' hands off pain meds. It was dying people and their people—dramatized, valorized—and the way they showed up for each other or didn't that mattered most in these daily stories.

Case Study with Roses

Once, years ago, a magazine published one of my essays. The day they posted it online, I read a comment below the link: "This is one of my favorite essays ever published by [this magazine]." My heart cartwheeled. And then, in real time, right as I was basking, another reader typed, "Really??? So *bleak!*" It reminded me of something Leo said to me when he was young. We were in our garden, which flourished because the previous owner—a minister whose research specialty was love—planted and tended it long before we came along. So well did he tend it that the garden lasted for years, flourishing long after he'd left. The garden bloomed with coneflower, cedar sage, phlox, and varieties of roses that ranged in color from velvet lipstick to goth white to prom dress pink. As Leo and I moved past one of the rose bushes, he stopped, looked at me—*Hey!*—and startled at his own insight. *It's like you, Mama. Soft but with prickles.*

He knew? I hadn't hidden it? I felt seen by my kid, flawed but fully. I don't want a relationship with anyone, least of all my kids, where they only see the prettiest petals. I hope my mother feels the same.

Case Study Without Imaginary Illness

Determined to detach love from illness, I would not give my kids a play-by-play when I had doctor's appointments. When I fell ill, I convalesced with my bedroom door open. I softened my voice when they burned from fever, but *also* when they were well.

Like my mom did, I talked about work. About students I adore. Lots of them. Colleagues. Stories about people telling stories, even. Because I worked from a home office long before a global pandemic made it the norm, I joked that every day of my kids' childhoods was *bring your kid to work day.*

Case Study with Hubris

I tried to get it exactly right. I offered stories of classroom dynamics, student awards, prison absurdities, and personal joys. An example, like my mom, I hoped, of a woman who was good at her job. A shared love of the people I love. What I consciously tried *not* to do is to focus incessantly on my kids' medical wellbeing. I felt the itch, but mostly resisted.

I "broke the generational cycle," as we say.

Fixed!

Leo, now in his twenties, confessed (gently) to me that he felt tired of hearing about my job. "Always *workworkwork*," was how he put it. He wished that I'd made myself more vulnerable. "I wish you'd talk less about work and share more of other things."

Shit.

Shit.

Sam still lived with me full-time during and after the divorce, so we endured the rough patches together. Through that hardship—that vulnerability his brother craved—we bonded intensely. But maybe not entirely in the way he needed. Last week during a late-night heart-to-heart, he mentioned (kindly) that he wished we had all been more courageous in our affections with each other. That we'd been braver about taking chances to connect as a family.

Shit.

Shit.

Who is this kid's mother?! How did I get it so wrong?

Case Study with Books

Leo, a big reader, was into science for years. Sharks, lizards, snakes, moths. One year, when school wasn't a good fit, I homeschooled him. It was in his science books that we first came across the axolotl: that goofy, alien, smiling lizard. Should someone chop off the salamander's arm, no big deal, she'll just begin the process of regeneration. Her magic allows her to use pluripotent cells to regenerate any other kind of cell the body requires: endoderm, exoderm, mesoderm, germ cell. In a lab, you can drop an axolotl's pluripotent cells on *any damaged area,* and it morphs into just what that wound needs. These cells are so restorative you can pluck from the arm to regrow the heart. You can slice from the heart to make brand new eyes.

I loved sharing such discoveries with the kids. I loved reading together, something I have no memories of as a kid. It felt good offering what my childhood lacked. I didn't realize doing so might prioritize mastery over connection. Excelling over coexisting.

Goddamn it.

Okay. But. What if we survive by converting what we get into what we need? I like to believe love works a little like that pluripotent cell. Apply anywhere, even a little or haphazardly, and because our lives depend on it, we can make something functional, if not downright beautiful out of it. Growing well, despite the wound.

Case Study with Charm

Years ago, back when I still had the stomach to interrogate abandonment, I drove five hundred miles to Arkansas to a dog training program housed in prisons across the rural South. By night, I settled into small cheap hotels beside fast-food chains. By day, I took a recorder and my questions to state prisons.

Arkansas is overrun with stray dogs, so every animal shelter but this one is a kill shelter. This means every dog they house is among the rare few that will survive. Not only are they spared death, but these dogs receive beautiful names in the Southern tradition: Axel Tucker, Bixby Williams, Boo Radley River, Gracie Change, and Socks Izard. They get second chances thanks to their incarcerated caretakers. The director of the dog program is emphatic: "This organization is for the dogs, the dogs, the dogs." She makes clear these facts: (1) "No offender gets paid for this work." (2) Career training is not the program's goal, though "offenders crave an *atta boy*," which she concedes they'll give from time to time. (3) "We are all about saving the dogs." She repeats this loudly and again in front of the women who train them inside their cells. I'm allowed to ask only about the dog training program, under the supervision of communications staff who stand beside me.

One trainer I meet, Tabitha, was tapped to work as the first dog handler. Tabitha wears frosted pink lipstick above a thin scar just below her lip and measures her every word. In the prison's cavernous gym, she maintains eye contact while, with the deftest of hand gestures, she silences a vocal German Shepard. The other women around the table, all of whom have dogs but none who share Tabitha's quiet command, admire her. A friend interrupts Tabitha to say, "She *always* doubts herself." Tabitha deflects the attention and explains the rocky start to her unpaid job as a trainer. Initially, the warden asked her to take the position, but she was so sure she'd screw up the budding program she cried herself to sleep. The next morning, puffy-eyed and pissed at herself for failing what she hadn't yet started, she told the warden: "I've thought about it, and I cannot take the job. Thanks, but no thanks."

The warden made her do it anyway, because it is prison, and sometimes in prison *offer* is another word for a *mandate*. Three years later, she's the most veteran trainer in the facility. Maybe Tabitha's warden was one of those employees who works hard within a broken system to make space for people's goodness. Maybe not. Either way, the system itself is louder and larger and more toxic than one kind person or their acts. Whatever Tabitha gains or gives, it is no thanks to Arkansas's prison system, which preferences the dogs over the humans who work with them and makes sure they know as much.

Tabitha explains that, for a dog to be eligible for adoption, he must pass the Canine Good Citizen test, which includes, among other directives: accept a friendly stranger, sit on command, and come when called. When a dog passes the test, he or she is eligible for adoption. Beyond that core training, Tabitha's personal program is playful, brilliant, and individualized. To *survive,* she says, a dog must not bite or shit on the floor. To *thrive,* "he must be irresistible." Tabitha's goal is to train her dogs to behave so meticulously, so etched in charm, "they'll never be put out again."

How charming do you have to be to avoid being put out?

Tabitha teaches her dogs to sing, to count, and to pray. When her dogs count to three, they do so through a staccato: bark, bark, bark. When she orders one to pray, he goes to a chair, lowers his head, crosses his paws, and embodies a quiet so still it passes as reverence. This is a bonus: She trained Gorgeous George, the slobbery Great Pyrenees whose days will be spent in a preschool classroom, to pull the covers over a napping child, to comfort kids with behavioral disorders, to wipe his own slobber on the towel that the kids hold beneath his mouth. (The command: *Wipe, George!*) Just as preschoolers endure a teacher washing their snotty noses, so too must Gorgeous George at the hands of preschoolers, because Tabitha wants him to find a permanent home. Irresistible. Un-put-outable.

Tabitha will be released in a few years, and when she is, she says, "All I want to do is drive around in my dad's truck and collect every abandoned dog I find." For now, she keeps a journal for every stray dog she trains. In teal ink she records the dog's daily progress, and the training tools she used to achieve them. Covered in collage and glitter, and filled with dated entries, the dog journals are part baby book, part training regiment, part testimonial of conjoined success. Whether she learned this devotion through example or its lack, she doesn't say. Either way, when the dog is adopted, she gifts the journal to the dog's new family, who could read the journal in so many ways:

- Ledger of historical fact. *8/7 Gorgeous George sat for kibble.*
- Escape. Writing in this journal beat chatting with Tabitha's cellie.
- Memoir. The person who wrote this journal understands

what it's like to lose your mom, your dad, your foster family, your bed.

- How-to-manual. The negative space around neglect is a blueprint for how to care.

Case Study with Plants

In the height of the pandemic, my friend Em asked me to care for a plant of hers before she made a cross-country move. So much did she love this desert plant that she drove it from North Carolina to South Dakota by itself so it would have a gentler ride. I met her, masked, in her mother's driveway, where she transferred the plant to my car, tucking in each leathery leaf before shutting the door. No mere plant, this was a gangly night-blooming Cereus who she named with the help of our friend Z., who was serving his nineteenth year in prison. Charles River's prickly-haired limbs hung at awkward angles. His crusty elbows (all five of them) bent in the most haphazard, non-negotiable way, taking up more room than seemed polite. This plant was no monstera.

Em once stayed up all night with Charles River as he produced his legendary twelve-hour nighttime bloom. She photographed all evening as its flower unfurled from a plant that had only five hours before looked indifferent, if not dead. And Em entrusted that miracle to my care! Never have I been more careful with a potted thing. I talked to this plant; I turned him toward the sun; I treated his plant-spreading with tender amusement, because I'd been shown this was a unique, beloved person, this plant. He was Em's Charles River who was peripherally adored by Z. It's like this, isn't it? The world handles more carefully things, and especially *people,* who are loudly loved. In the way a package marked "Fragile" travels with relative care, overtly adored humans are marked "Special," and we instinctively honor that.

Case Study with Pam

Z. knows about being loudly loved. I asked him if I could mention his mom in my work and he said, "Please do. Everyone should know about Pam." I met her during a public reading of student writing. In the large, softly lit room, Pam stood among a crowd of hundreds to introduce herself as Z.'s mom, six feet tall, or so it seemed. Everyone remained seated, but she stood in the second row, center. She told the crowd of several hundred: *He's a beautiful writer. I'm so proud of him.* It wasn't a mushy proclamation by any measure; you heard steel in her voice, the same steel Z. used to build community inside prison, because the action part of love comes natural to him, having lived under its force field his entire life. That was her first hello, but we'd hear from Pam often. Everyone in Z.'s orbit did.

Pam died before Z. left prison. Six weeks before she passed, she sent this email to the organization I work with, likely similar to thousands she'd sent to others during his incarceration:

> Hi, this is Z.'s mom. As you probably know, Z. has been moved to Goodhue County Jail. It's a restrictive place and he can only write with pencil and paper. (2 pencils for 75 cents and 5 sheets of paper for $1.) I cannot send or bring him books. He did talk to the Program Director there and she said he could only receive books sent by [your organization]—with prior approval from her, and not too many at a time. With him confined to his cell most of the day, all he has is reading and writing to pass the time. He can only have his pencils sharpened by staff in the short time he is out of his cell.
>
> Let me know what we can do . . .

By "what we can do," she meant, *I will not let up until I see that he has books.* Go ahead and replace "books" with a list of endless needs. Twenty years of them, all complicated to solve. *I will not let up until he has glasses, a doctor's appointment, a hearing, ______, ______, ______.* I will not let up until he comes home. Or until I am gone. She did not. Pam Caligiuri never let up.

Case Study with Strangers

It's fall, the last golden-crisp day in Minnesota when I'm walking my now-senior dog, Toby. My kids are grown. The time for connecting and correcting mistakes with all those I love is fleeting. I feel older lately, like I'm beginning the end of something, and that makes me sad. Also, I don't love to see my reflection in store windows. But the air is cool, the sun is warm, and my two feet and Toby's four paws fall in sync after eleven years walking side by side, and we're in our stride and the woman having breakfast with a friend outside of Groundswell Café yells as we pass, "You look amazing!" to my dog, because he is freshly groomed and dog-smiling beside me, though he can't talk, and so I answer for him, "He says thanks, and so does your bacon," and she laughs and shouts louder, "I meant *you*!"

Case Studies, the Postscripts

Gorgeous George, Tabitha's Great Pyrenees, probably goes to work with the preschoolers each day and licks the peanut butter off the faces of the children. Just kidding, he would never. Little Josie, who can't sit still in the circle, climbs on him when the teacher isn't looking. George lets her forty pounds squirm till she's worked the wiggles out. When his person says, "George, come!" he lifts his body and galumphs forward. She will ask him to sit, which he will do so quickly and well you can't believe it. The children line up behind him. His person lets him lead the line outside to recess. The door opens and they all file out. After that, they walk back in, wash up, and have snacks. *Wipe, George, wipe!* They take turns holding his cloth. At the end of the day, the children climb in the cars and travel to their homes, and Gorgeous George gets in the car and goes to his.

Home is where he lives now. Tabitha is a smell he remembers, buried somewhere in his muscles when he *moves* or when he *sits*, and especially when he *stays*.

* * *

Once plant-spreading Charles River was back with Em—which is to say out of my care and back home—his limbs grew wilder. Em trimmed them and set the cuttings in a jar filled with water. She's a propagator if ever I saw one. While she waited for Z. to come home, Charles River's cuttings sprouted baby-fine roots. One day Em got the call. As she'd planned, she took Charles River's rooted limb, placed it in a pot with black soil, patted it down, watered it, and brought it to a dinner, which as it happens, was a welcome home party for Z., after twenty-one years locked away. His girlfriend, whose strength reminds me of Pam's, decorated the table, which sat in the back of a restaurant, under a row of pendant lights. Wine glasses reflected the tea candles' flames. Origami swans, small jars of wildflowers, and the sun setting through the window made of that corner both party and prayer.

Z. had never seen Charles River in person, but he'd heard lots of stories by phone. He knew exactly who Em was holding when he saw her walk in with the green tendril in her outstretched hand.

* * *

I remember it in my lungs. I am five years old, at my mother's feet at four a.m., before she leaves for work. We're in the bathroom while she unrolls plastic rollers from her hair, unraveling each one with care. The room is clouded with cigarette smoke—Vantage UltraLights 100. I'm curled in a blanket, sitting beside the electric heater; her voice is quiet and kind. I have no future, no past, only this cocoon. She zips closed her makeup bag, leaves the bathroom for her bedroom. I get up to follow and, maybe because of the heat or the cigarette smoke or the early morning hour, or maybe because I don't want it to end, my neck flushes hot and my lips go numb, and I faint. When I wake, it's to her cool hands on my forehead, and she stays a little longer.

* * *

My wildly different sons are both brave enough to share their disappointments with me. I'm proud of that. They inherit all I may have gifted them, and all my giving has taken. My *work-workwork*, my adoration for them. Dogs. Possibly a bouquet of gerbera daisies, when I earn them for once, by dying. This much, I hope most of all: a commitment to trying. May whatever love I give, and whatever love I misapplied, flourish in them and theirs—stubbornly like Pam's, joyful like a nighttime burst, prickly and enduring, like an old rose bush, rooted deep. May it sustain the strongest of pulses in their kin and theirs, so sturdy and sure that no one remembers where it started or how, only that that it beats inside them, and will continue.

Notes

An Inquiry into Epigenetics

33 ***The scientists are saying*** Ewen Callaway, "Fearful Memories Haunt Mouse Descendants," *Nature,* December 1, 2013, https://doi.org/10.1038/nature.2013.14272

36 ***Anything that grows*** Gabriel A. Orenstein and Lindsay Lewis, "Erikson's Stages of Psychosocial Development," National Library of Medicine, updated November 7, 2022, https://www.ncbi.nlm.nih.gov/books/NBK556096/.

38 ***leads to discernable changes*** University of British Columbia, "Parents' stress leaves lasting marks on children's genes, researchers find," ScienceDaily, September 9, 2011, https://www.sciencedaily.com/releases/2011/08/110830144630.htm.

Open Window, Burning House

43 ***I pass walls covered in visual art*** Reidar Faanes, interview with the author, October 27, 2014.

45 ***The Inmate: Who Is He*** "Welcome to Halden Prison: Punishment That Works, Change That Lasts," PowerPoint Presentation, 2014.

46 ***When men come to prison*** Jan Strømnes, interview with the author, October 27, 2014.

The Wildest Show

69 ***Angola Prison exists*** Angola Prison Rodeo, souvenir booklet, 2015.

72 ***average sentence length*** Justin Hosbey, "Angola Prison's Black Ecologies," *Environment and Planning F: Philosophy, Theory, Models, Methods and Practice,* 2025, https://doi.org/10.1177/26349825241296077.

78 ***Seventy-five percent of folks who enter*** Caroline Wolf Harlow, "Education and Correctional Populations," Bureau of Justice Statistics, revised April 15, 2003, https://bjs.ojp.gov/content/pub/pdf/ecp.pdf.

78 ***The average reading level*** Public records request, Louisiana State Prison, July 4, 2024.

78 ***In Louisiana such facts*** Public records request.

78 ***More than half of all imprisoned men*** Leah Wang, "Chronic Punishment: The Unmet Health Needs of People in State Prisons," Press release, Prison Policy Initiative, June 2022, https://www.prisonpolicy.org/reports/chronicpunishment.html#mentalhealth.

78 ***Black men at Angola*** Public records request.

78 ***One in every twenty-eight children*** "Collateral Costs: Incarceration's Effect on Economic Mobility," Pew Charitable Trusts, 21, https://www.pewtrusts.org/-/media/3975EB366428437FADA60843AA02C2FC.ashx.

Human Ecology

84 ***Former warden, minister*** Arne Kvernvik Nilsen, interview with the author, October 21, 2014.

86 ***In* Nature as Measure** Wes Jackson, *Nature as Measure: The Selected Essays of Wes Jackson* (Counterpoint, 2011).

86 ***Call it a camp for criminals*** Nilsen, interview.

87 ***You want me to make someone*** Tom Eberhardt, interview with the author, October 23, 2014.

Attention

89 ***Passengers?*** "Chicago-Bound Train Kills Man Near Detroit," *Chicago Tribune*, February 12, 2009, https://www.chicagotribune.com/2009/02/12/chicago-bound-train-kills-man-near-detroit/.

96 ***Attention, taken to its highest degree*** Simone Weil, *Gravity and Grace* (Routledge, 2002), 117.

Watched

119 ***There exists a man*** "Bylund Lars (Sweden)," staff page, Before the Congress, accessed November 5, 2024, https://wsec.kz/staff-member/bylund-lars-sweden/.

121 ***Nathaniel-of-the-Musical*** Lasse Andresen and Nathaniel, interview with the author, October 27, 2014.

126 ***The week I arrive at Halden*** "Halden Prison," *Cathedrals of Culture*, directed by Karim Aïnouz, Michael Glawogger, Michael Madsen et al. (2014).

Night Cows

182 ***In this unnatural state of isolation*** Peter Libbey and Jason Farago, "The World's Great Photographers, Many Stuck Inside, Have Snapped," *New York Times*, updated September 21, 2021, https://www.nytimes.com/2020/04/02/arts/design/instagram-photographers-coronavirus.html.

Music in the Midway

194 ***Americans have long been trained*** Ibram X. Kendi, *How to Be an Antiracist* (One World, 2019), 28.

199 ***adrienne maree brown asserts*** adrienne maree brown, *Emergent Strategy: Shaping Change, Changing Worlds* (AK Press, 2017), 140-50.

200 ***brown says in her book*** adrienne maree brown, *We Will Not Cancel Us: And Other Dreams of Transformative Justice* (AK Press, 2020), 70.

Acknowledgments

When you take a decade or so to finish a book, you find a lot of help along the way. I've been fed, nourished, housed, claimed, calmed, bolstered, energized, inspired, taught, and loved by a massive family of good humans, all of whom had a role in making belonging, and this book, possible.

Individual essays or versions of them appeared in the journals below. I'm grateful to editors Derek Askey, David Lynn, Scott Gast, Roxane Gay, Kim Groninga, Nancy Holochwost, Sy Safransky, Kathryn Savage, Andrew Snee, for making my essays better, and for supporting this country's literary ecosystem.

Arts & Letters: "Candling Delicious"
Orion: "Human Ecology"
The Sun: "The Library"
North American Review: "Attention"
The Sun: "Next of Kin"
Kenyon Review: "An Inquiry Into Epigenetics"
Pushcart Prize Anthology, The Sun: "Night Cows"
The Rumpus: "Leaving Delicious" (Published as "Of Farmers and Fathers")
The Sun: "Surrogates"
Defunct: "FWD"
Water~Stone Review: "The End of the World As We Know It" (Published as "Just the Song")

I'd like to thank the Jerome Foundation for supporting travel to Norway, Arkansas, and Louisiana. Bread Loaf and the Rona Jaffe Foundation for a Bread Loaf–Rona Jaffe Scholarship. Thank you to the good people of the great state of Minnesota who support the legacy amendment, which opens doors to art, thriving, and a creative community unparalleled, a community that inspires and sustains me.

I owe tremendous gratitude to my agent, Jennifer Thompson, whose gentle insistence carried me through when I doubted. Ronald L. Greer, vibrant editor and OG order-er, thank you. Thank you to the entire Milkweed team: Lauren, Tessa, Craig, Katie, Anessa, Morgan, Madi, Morissa, Alex, Sean, Zoey, Bri, Jane, Colleen, Sheena, Daniel, and especially Mary Austin Speaker, my editor, for believing in this book, for seeing care in my work, and for caring to make it beautiful.

My MPWW family who raised each other's words, and the rooms we inhabit together: K, L, M., J., Don, Ghost, Fresh, Woods, Tate, Chang, South Side, 2Tone, Aloha, Ms. B., Coty, Linda, Bailey, Fourteen, C.E., Davi, Ebi, Tate, Donny U, Collins, Rod, Dallas, Jesse, Mr. Thomas, Jazz, Red, Redd, Antonio, Kev, Sarith, Von, Kennedy, David, Will, Warren, Louise, Glitter Squirrel, Paulo, B., Bino, Fong Francis, Chris, Zeke: Thank you all for the joy and the gravity you have brought to my life, and to the way I understand community. Thank you for showing me what words are capable of when the stakes are high. Thank you to beloved MPWW instructors Deborah Appleman, Ryan Berg, Heidi Czerwiec, Michael Kleber-Diggs, Amy Fladeboe, David Lawrence Grant, Mary

Stein, April Gibson, Halee Kirkwood, Alice Paige, Kristin Collier, Abbey Mei Otis, Jeannine Ouellette, Junuada Petrus Nasah, Beau RaRa, Erin Sharkey, Sun Yung Shin (+Julian and the cabin), Sam Stokley, Bionik, Elizabeth Tannen, Michael Torres, plus Ruby Haack and Ari Tison: some of the most outstanding writers and educators on the planet. Mike Alberti, Su Hwang, Rachel Moritz, capable and talented friends and colleagues who make our community sturdy and pitch in when I need time away to write, thank you; I can't imagine a better team. Thank you, loudly, to the Basement Squad who built a beautiful foundation that endures and influences my work and world: Wendy Brown Baez, Bill Breen, Dain Edwards, Peter Pearson, Nico Taranovsky, Nell Ubbelohde, and Kelly Hansen Maher, whose vision is artful and uncompromising, just like her poems and friendship.

The world gifted me devoted teachers and mentors. I'm grateful for the rest of my days and through every page to Rita Nance, Steve Almond, Robin Hemley, Will Jennings, Stephen Coyne, Ed Mazeika, Lawrence Sutin, Robert Vivian, Jess Row, Aminatta Forna, Lauren Markham, and David Jauss. Thank you to teachers of all grades everywhere for the work you do and for the books that will someday be written because of you.

Thank you to writer friends whose brilliance illuminates a path I aspire to walk: Inara Verzemnieks, Lesley Nneka Arimah, Kelly Jo. Thanks to those who read drafts of this work throughout the years: Jennifer Koski, Sara Reish Desmond, Peg Ludtke, Mary Stein, stalwart readers from the earliest day. Robin MacArthur, whose editorial eye is as loving as it is wise and whose voice on and off the page transports me to the beating heart. Bug Out Baggers MKD, Erin Sharkey, Heidi Czerwiec, Katrina Vandenberg: My bag is (re)packed and you made that, plus this book, better. Good witches: Kirsten Fischer, Mackenzie Epping, Rachel Moritz, Angela Pelster-Weibe, thank you for your insight and generosity in reading and in crises—always, often—for bringing sturdiness to these essays and to my days.

Thanks to friends who've championed my book and the people I care about: Chris Fischbach, Hans Weyandt, Steve Horowitz. Philip, for light-chasing and altitude during writing breaks. Emily Baxter, thought partner, propagator, master photographer—thank you for all the bright ideas and beauty you bring to my life and others'. Chani Reese, I will always have a room for you. Tessa Anttila, a poet once told me it takes fifty pages to make a spine. For me, it took you. Gina Nacey, thank you, friend, for loving my kids, for loving me, and for (very literally) walking through the hardest days beside me.

Bill and Jerry, in memoriam, thank you both for helping me grow in sweet and complicated ways. I'm sorry we can't smooth out the knots in this lifetime. Krissy and Amy, I'm grateful I got the middle seat so I had you on my left and right. Mom, thank you for showing me the importance of other people's stories and for listening better than anyone else, so I believed mine mattered, too.

Elliot and Ollie, thank you for supporting my writing with grace and maturity from your earliest days to now. You are the reason I want to get it right—the words and this life. Wherever I live, and even after I'm gone, you are my home.

Jennifer Eli Bowen is the founder and artistic director of the Minnesota Prison Writing Workshop, an organization that brings art and community into state prisons. Her writing appears in the Pushcart Prize anthology, *Orion*, *The Sun*, *Kenyon Review*, *Iowa Review*, and *The Rumpus* and has been anthologized in *The Sentences That Create Us: Crafting a Writer's Life in Prison* and *Buffalo Cactus and Other New Stories from the Southwest*. Her work has been honored with the Pushcart Prize, The Arts & Letters Susan Atefat Prize for Nonfiction, and the Tim McGinnis Award. Bowen has two sons, two dogs, and lives in St. Paul, Minnesota, down the block from ghosts of ancestors she never met.

Founded as a nonprofit organization in 1980, Milkweed Editions is an independent publisher. Our mission is to identify, nurture, and publish transformative literature, and build an engaged community around it.

We are based in Bde Óta Othúŋwe (Minneapolis) in Mní Sota Makhóčhe (Minnesota), the traditional homeland of the Dakhóta and Anishinaabe (Ojibwe) people and current home to many thousands of Dakhóta, Ojibwe, and other Indigenous people, including four federally recognized Dakhóta nations and seven federally recognized Ojibwe nations.

We believe all flourishing is mutual, and we envision a future in which all can thrive. Realizing such a vision requires reflection on historical legacies and engagement with current realities. We humbly encourage readers to do the same.

milkweed.org

Milkweed Editions, an independent nonprofit literary publisher, gratefully acknowledges sustaining support from our board of directors, the McKnight Foundation, the National Endowment for the Arts, and many generous contributions from foundations, corporations, and thousands of individuals—our readers. This activity is made possible by the voters of Minnesota through a Minnesota State Arts Board Operating Support grant, thanks to a legislative appropriation from the Arts and Cultural Heritage Fund.

Interior design by Mary Austin Speaker
Typeset in Arno Pro

Arno was designed by Robert Slimbach.
Slimbach named this typeface after the river that runs through Florence, Italy. Arno draws inspiration from a variety of typefaces created during the Italian Renaissance; its italics were inspired by the calligraphy and printing of Ludovico degli Arrighi.